Formative Assessment in United States Classrooms

Cathy Box

Formative Assessment in United States Classrooms

Changing the Landscape of Teaching and Learning

Cathy Box
Lubbock Christian University
Lubbock, TX, USA

ISBN 978-3-030-03091-9   ISBN 978-3-030-03092-6 (eBook)
https://doi.org/10.1007/978-3-030-03092-6

Library of Congress Control Number: 2018962863

© The Editor(s) (if applicable) and The Author(s) 2019
This work is subject to copyright. All rights are solely and exclusively licensed by the Publisher, whether the whole or part of the material is concerned, specifically the rights of translation, reprinting, reuse of illustrations, recitation, broadcasting, reproduction on microfilms or in any other physical way, and transmission or information storage and retrieval, electronic adaptation, computer software, or by similar or dissimilar methodology now known or hereafter developed.
The use of general descriptive names, registered names, trademarks, service marks, etc. in this publication does not imply, even in the absence of a specific statement, that such names are exempt from the relevant protective laws and regulations and therefore free for general use.
The publisher, the authors and the editors are safe to assume that the advice and information in this book are believed to be true and accurate at the date of publication. Neither the publisher nor the authors or the editors give a warranty, express or implied, with respect to the material contained herein or for any errors or omissions that may have been made. The publisher remains neutral with regard to jurisdictional claims in published maps and institutional affiliations.

Cover credit: © Nick Measures / iStock / gettyimages

This Palgrave Macmillan imprint is published by the registered company Springer Nature Switzerland AG
The registered company address is: Gewerbestrasse 11, 6330 Cham, Switzerland

Acknowledgments

This book emerged as the result of a manuscript I published in the October 2015 issue of the *American Educational Research Journal* entitled "A case study of teacher personal practice assessment theories and complexities of implementing formative assessment." Publication of that manuscript and of this monograph would have been most difficult without the advice and council of my friend, colleague, and mentor, Dr. Gerald Skoog, a Paul Whitfield Horn Professor Emeritus at Texas Tech University. I can never thank him enough for his patience, wisdom, and guidance.

I would also like to thank my daughter, Nikki Tekell, math teacher extraordinaire, for providing thoughtful and challenging feedback that grounded the narrative in reality, and my sister, Connie Harrington, for her extensive research into our family history of educators. I also thank Dr. Kregg Fehr, Professor of History at Lubbock Christian University for reviewing my chapter on the history of assessment and accountability in the United States, and my deepest gratitude for her review and constructive feedback also extends to Betty Stennett, my former teaching partner-in-crime who now works as a Curriculum Developer for Biological Sciences Curriculum Study (BSCS).

Lastly, I want to thank my husband, Ray, and the rest of my family for their love, enthusiastic support, and enduring patience during the writing process. I wouldn't have had the courage to climb this mountain without them.

Contents

1 The Evolution of Assessment and Accountability in the United States   1

2 The Power of Formative Assessment   25

3 Embedding Formative Assessment: A Peek Inside the Black Box   49

4 The Classroom Teacher   75

5 The Professional Development of Teachers   105

6 A Renewed Vision for Professional Development   131

7 Systemic Change   155

Index   177

LIST OF FIGURES

Fig. 2.1	A visual representation of the learning bridge as described by Furtak (2005)	32
Fig. 4.1	Cornett's (1990) curriculum development model based on the impact of PPTs	82
Fig. 4.2	Assessment Development Model based on the impact of PPATs and contextual elements. Modified from Cornett's (1990) curriculum development model	83
Fig. 4.3	Assessment Development Model—Phoebe	86
Fig. 4.4	Assessment Development Model—Mary	92
Fig. 4.5	Assessment Development Model—Monica	96
Fig. 6.1	Hypothetical behavior over time graph	142

LIST OF ILLUSTRATIONS

Illustration 5.1 Job application denoting 2- and 4-year certificates 107
Illustration 5.2 Texas 2-year teaching certificate 108
Illustration 5.3 Texas 2-year certification exam report 109

List of Tables

Table 3.1	Rubric to determine attributes of formative assessment	51
Table 3.2	Demographic information of Phoebe's students	52
Table 3.3	Demographic information of Mary's students	60
Table 3.4	Demographic information for Monica's students	66
Table 4.1	Assessment Development Model summary	100
Table 5.1	Twenty-first-century competencies, skills, and dimensions for students	125
Table 7.1	A comparison of a grade vs. learning mentality	159

CHAPTER 1

The Evolution of Assessment and Accountability in the United States

Since the inception of organized education in the United States, social, political, and economic factors have shaped our school system into one that is firmly entrenched into a structure that is teacher centered and instructivistic, so common that it is what we refer to as traditional instruction. This system-driven model of education has found itself at odds with what we know about the nature of learners and learning, leaving it wanting. This chapter provides a historical context of events, circumstances, and conditions that situated us where we are today and the impact they have had on learners and learning.

AMERICAN SCHOOLS: HISTORY AND CONTEXT

Colonial period (1600–1776). Education in Colonial America during the seventeenth and eighteenth centuries was heavily influenced by cultural norms that colonists brought with them from Europe and was largely dependent on social class and wealth. Formal schooling in the 13 colonies was often tuition based and was intended to provide classical training (primarily to boys of wealthy families) in literacy and numeracy. Education was not systematic, organized, or compulsory, and opportunities varied greatly from colony to colony. Additionally, much of the educational content was religious, and its purpose was to prepare individuals to live as godly citizens and to prosper in the growing economy. As a general rule, teachers were young, single men in transition to more stable careers. There were no formal

© The Author(s) 2019
C. Box, *Formative Assessment in United States Classrooms*,
https://doi.org/10.1007/978-3-030-03092-6_1

academic requirements for becoming a teacher; most were selected based on their moral fiber and adherence to local religious values rather than for their ability to teach (Drury & Baer, 2011, p. 2). Laws and customs forbade teaching slaves and free African Americans, but primary education was available to most other white children through Dame Schools, run by women of high moral character but often limited education.

During this time, immigrants continued to arrive by ship and the new world had a wealth of raw materials that needed to be developed by skilled workers, however. Therefore, some boys (and later girls) were trained on the job through apprenticeships. The system of apprenticeships provided young boys the opportunity to learn a trade from a "master" and within seven years have the skills needed to begin one's own business. The master also trained the young man in matters of faith and religion in order to prepare him to live a pious life. Apprenticeships benefited society in two ways; they helped the economy grow, and they prepared children for vocation. Another common practice of the times was for families to provide informal vocational training for children at home that provided them with the knowledge and skills they needed for survival, in this case surviving and conquering the wilderness. Although records of assessment practices from both formal and informal education in colonial America are absent, we can surmise that they were based on evidence of mastery of the skill being learned and that the teacher, master, or parent adjusted instruction in practical ways until his pupil had the knowledge and skills required to successfully complete the task.

Ultimately, educational opportunities were hit and miss at best, and over time, colonist began to see a more concerted need to provide education for all of its citizenry that served the practical needs of humanity and began to realize the value of learning as a tool for gaining independence (Spring, 2001, p. 13).

Early National period (1776–1840). Soon after America fought for and gained independence from Great Britain, the newly formed republic realized that if it was to survive, thrive, and become a great nation, then its citizens must be educated—all of them. This philosophy was strongly promoted by Thomas Jefferson, Benjamin Franklin, Noah Webster, and other theorists in the late eighteenth century who began to cast a vision for American education. One of the first significant attempts to organize education in the United States occurred in 1779 when Thomas Jefferson introduced into the Virginia legislature a "Bill for the More General Diffusion of Knowledge" with three assumptions: (1) republican government and democratic decision making required an educated and literate citizenry, (2) education should be a political function and not a religious one, and (3) educational control should be visited in state governments (Gutek, 1991, p. 33). In this document, we see the first seeds of accountability. Jefferson wrote:

> Over every ten of these schools an overseer shall be appointed annually by the aldermen at their first meeting, eminent for his learning, integrity, and fidelity to the commonwealth, whose business and duty it shall be, from time to time, to appoint a teacher to each school, who shall give assurance of fidelity to the commonwealth, and to remove him as he shall see cause; to visit every school once in every half year at the least; to examine the scholars; see that any general plan of reading and instruction recommended by the visitors of William and Mary college shall be observed; and to superintend the conduct of the teacher in every thing relative to his school. (Gutek, p. 48)

Notice that teachers were evaluated but not the students or their academic achievement. The bill called for evidence that the "scholar" had a general plan of instruction and that he was conducting himself in a proper manner. Though not a stringent and well-defined plan for accountability, it was a start.

Although the founding fathers recognized the need for organized education, industrialism consumed the country's youth, and most children received minimum schooling, if any. Many children continued to learn from their parents at home or through apprenticeships. In response, Joseph Lancaster introduced a system of education in which large groups of children could be educated cheaply. However, the quality of education was questionable. In this system, 200 to 1000 students were gathered in one room and seated in rows of ten. The adult schoolmaster, who may or may not have been qualified, taught the brighter students (monitors or prefects) who then taught the students in their rows. Other students were used as monitors to track attendance, to assess and promote students, to distribute supplies, and so on—hence the name "monitorial schools." Due to the structure of the system, teachers were relegated to the position of organizer, and students learned through rote memorization, drill, and practice. The process of teaching was of military precision, automatized and formalized, leaving little room for creativity and innovation. This was one of the first examples of mass education. The curriculum focused on literacy, numeracy, Christian principles, and civic duty related to patriotism of the newly formed republic. African Americans had greater access to formal instruction in the North, but education for Southern African Americans was still forbidden in an attempt to protect the institution of slavery. Monitorial schools were short lived and eventually replaced by a more "modern" system of education involving grouping students by age and using the lecture method of instruction instead of monitors and prefects.

Common School period (1840–1880). Continued recognition that the health of the nation depended on education for all of its populace gave rise to the "common school"—a precursor of public school education as we know it today. Horace Mann (1796–1859), considered the Father of the Common School movement, proposed a system of education that was free, universal, and non-sectarian. The first common schools served elementary white children and focused on literacy, numeracy, and citizenship. The movement grew throughout the early nineteenth century, concurrent with westward expansion and an influx of European immigrants. Rural common schools were often one-room schoolhouses with multiple grade levels taught in the same room. The teacher was largely responsible for oversight and was given much autonomy with scarce accountability. Common schools in urban areas were more structured—overseen by a board of trustees and governed by a principal, superintendent, and teachers—and began to align students by age as well as standardize and sequence the curriculum. Accountability was still limited to making sure that students attended school and teachers did what they were supposed to do. After the Civil War as the United States became more industrialized, many schools in large urban areas adopted the factory model of organization while the one-room schoolhouse remained a fixture in the rural areas of the South, Midwest, and Western states. Southern states enacted Jim Crow laws that legalized segregation—claiming "separate but equal" opportunities for recently freed slaves. During this time, taxpayers began to pay for public education, attendance became compulsory, and standardization became the goal in order to accommodate the great number of students in attendance and to ensure quality instruction.

By the mid-nineteenth century, the elementary classroom was firmly established in the ideology and practice of instructionism. Instructionism, a phrase coined by Seymour Papert (1993), refers to a transmission model of communication in which a teacher instructs by transmitting facts to a passively receptive student. In this traditional vision of schooling, the goal is to get facts and procedures into students' heads and then test them to see what they have acquired. It is often referred to as teacher-centered or an instructivist approach to teaching and learning. Students were expected to listen to their teacher talk, take notes, memorize, recite, and work quietly and independently at their desks. They were to face the front, respond in unison or raise their hand to answer a question, and speak only when spoken to. Assessments were generally oral recitations based on students' ability to memorize, and errors often resulted in punishment. Ranking was the typical method of grading both for the recitations and for formal examinations and was conducted by the master of the school or by an outside board (Cureton, 1971, p. 2). Schools supported by public money demanded the right to determine if the money was well spent, and in addition to examining buildings, administration, and school records, some inspections included an examination of the teachers and students as well. In some districts, superintendents held public meetings where the teacher was interviewed and questioned, resulting in retention or dismissal.

During that time a group of school reformers hoped to replace traditional classroom practices with a more learner-centered approach to learning as introduced by Swiss educator Johann Pestalozzi (1746–1827). Pestalozzi, considered the "Father of Modern Education," popularized the first systematic method of instruction that was learner centered. He asserted that education should be centered on the child not the curriculum and that children learned through experiences and discovery, advocating for an inductive method of inquiry. This was perhaps one of the first attempts to combine psychology and the understanding of how students build knowledge with the process of teaching and learning. One might consider his approach the beginning seeds of constructivism—a philosophy of education that contends that learning is an active process where learners build on existing knowledge. This philosophy of learning was also embraced by other school reformers who recognized the potential for moving away from instructionism with its automation and dull recitations that had become the norm in American schools, and a number of "practice schools" using progressive methods emerged as a result.

> The major impact of Pestalozzian theory was its emphasis on relating instruction in the early years to objects in the real world, on learning by doing, and on the importance of activity, as opposed to sitting at a desk. By the end of the nineteenth century, the Pestalozzian practices had become an important part of progressive instructional theory, and by the twentieth century they were an important part of elementary classroom practice. (Spring, 2001, p. 145)

Pestalozzi had a profound effect on education, and his theories materialized through the work of reformers such as Edward Sheldon, Francis Parker, and most notably John Dewey.

Dewey (1859–1952) was by far one of the most prominent and outspoken proponents of a system of education that viewed learning as a communal, experiential endeavor. He promoted the idea that schools could serve society by helping students learn to solve problems collaboratively and use testing to validate their ideas, a form of the scientific method he called the "complete act of thought" (Gutek, 1991, p. 257). Through the University of Chicago in 1896, he developed his famous Laboratory School, sometimes referred to as his experimental school (1896–1904) to put his theories into practice and in the spirit of practice-centered inquiry (PCI)—to test them. Students were expected to interact socially and work together to solve problems, creating an atmosphere of community. Knowledge and skills related to various content areas were developed and used in the service of problem solving, an example of learning in context rather than in isolation. This social experiment was short-lived, but nevertheless laid a foundation for reform that provided new ways to think about curriculum, child development and learning, and learner-centered instruction. His ideas, however, were antithetical to behaviorist views of learning that had been popularized by psychologists such as William James (1842–1910) and Edward Thorndike (1874–1949) and struggled to gain purchase within existing systems. But fortunately, although teacher-centered practices continued to dominate instruction, an alternate view of education and the role that students and teachers could play was proposed, modeled, and reproduced in many classrooms across the country.

Although constructivist practices made modest inroads into school systems due to the influence of Pestalozzi, Dewey, and other reformers, much of the country was still deeply entrenched in instructionism, and teaching and learning continued to be heavily influenced by external, systemic needs. Up to this point, assessment practices in the classroom relied on memorization and verbal responses that were used to determine achievement. One of the first instances of written student assessment came in Boston in 1845 when the school committee attempted to assess levels of student knowledge through written questions for analysis and reporting purposes. However, Boston schools had many students, and Mann, as secretary of the Massachusetts Board of Education, was faced with the challenge of monitoring their learning and thus sought to standardize testing in order to rank and compare students. By his own account, Mann predicted that "the mode of examination by printed questions and written answers…will constitute a new era in the history of…schools" (Mann, as cited in Madaus, Russell, & Higgins, 2009, p. 117). These were prophetic words, indeed. This mode of standardized assessment paralleled a societal movement toward standardization in industry throughout New England and had a significant influence on practice in American schools thereafter.

True to his philosophy of transparency, Mann asserted that test scores should be published in local newspapers in order to hold schools and teachers accountable. He attributed low scores to the teacher, rather than the student, believing that all students could learn given the right opportunities. This belief prevailed for many years until the early twentieth century when IQ tests were developed, and results were used as evidence that the innate intelligence of some students was low. This theory shifted the blame of poor learning from the teacher to the student and led to a system of tracking students. Tracking students had detrimental effects for minorities and other non-English speakers as it depended on normative standards to compare students to one another, rather than on mastery or performance standards that might provide opportunities for all students to be successful (Madaus et al., 2009, p. 124).

During this era, curriculum focused on literacy, numeracy, history, and geography. Leaders were still more concerned with how to structure and fund schools, what curriculum should be taught, how teachers should be prepared, and what textbooks should be required. Little thought was given to understanding the nature of students and what they needed in order to be successful, and then making sure that it worked (i.e., assessing outcomes).

Progressive period (1880–1920). Some of the first records of assessing outcomes and using data to improve schools can be attributed to William Torrey Harris (1835–1909). William Harris, a leader in education and an advocate of the free common public school, served as the superintendent of schools in St. Louis, Missouri, from 1868 to 1880 and the US Commissioner of Education from 1889 to 1906. He is primarily known for his contributions to philosophy and to the theory and practice of education (Leidecker, 1946). However, "his use of educational statistics, including student data, provided a method for describing his district and demonstrating its problems and needs. He was a major proponent of the survey movement for studying and comparing school districts. His scientific approach to the study of education helped organize and systematize it as a social science" (Hassenpflug & Hassenpflug, 2010).

By the early 1900s, the scientific approach to education began to take root and shape practice. In 1904, Thorndike of Columbia University published the *Theory of Mental and Social Measurements* in which he argued that "facts of human nature can be made the material for quantitative science" (p. v). This and subsequent work by Thorndike advanced an administrative progressivism that was strictly utilitarian (Labaree, 2005), and focused on governance, organization, and efficiency.

During the Progressive period, educational systems were characterized by a top-down organizational hierarchy that placed "experts" in charge, depended on measurement of efficiency, and laid claims to a meritocracy—the idea that each individual's social and occupational position is determined by individual merit not political or economic influence (Spring, 2001, p. 287). In addition to Thorndike, the movement was strongly influenced by Frederick W. Taylor (1856–1915), a high-profile engineer whose book *The Principles of Scientific Management* systemized shop management in ways that would reduce cost and increase production—a theory referred to as Taylorism. In the Taylorism era, the school's role was to function like an efficient factory to educate the masses and to be run by professional managers and experts. It was founded on the premise that all students should be given an equal opportunity to learn. They hoped to replace unfair hierarchies that had arisen due to social class and wealth with a system that was scientifically objective. Standardization flourished during the Taylorism era, and many of the effects are still felt today. Teacher training, certification and evaluation, merit pay, school finance procedures, evaluation of students through testing, hiring procedures, attendance records, and other standardized procedures can be directly attributed to Frederick W. Taylor.

Classroom instruction was also subject to Taylorism. Although some schools subscribed to the Pestalozzian theory of teaching and learning, most urban schools still employed a very teacher-centered, one-size-fits-all approach to instruction. Rows of desks bolted to the floor faced a teacher's desk and blackboard. Schools were age graded, curriculum was standardized, and expectations for advancement were lock-step with age. Drill and practice homework was frequently assigned, and parents were notified of student progress through report cards. Classrooms were crowded with often 40–50 students in a class. Teachers were expected to teach content from several different areas (for which they were not trained), and many teachers did not have any formal training whatsoever, so they relied heavily on textbooks to teach the curriculum. Additionally, direct instruction, memorization and recitation, and uniform assignments, reporting of grades, and passing standards simply made the process of handling so many students much more manageable given their circumstances.

The structure of rural schools, on the other hand, looked much different. They were usually not age-graded which led to crowded conditions as students of all ages were put in a single room. They were often housed in older buildings and garnered less financial support, were taught by less qualified teachers, and suffered from a lack of supplies and quality textbooks. However, according to Barabara Finkelstine who examined over 1000 classrooms of the mid to late nineteenth century, the mode of instruction was the same in urban and rural schools alike. "North and south, east and west, in rural schools as well as urban schools, teachers assigned lessons, asked questions and created standards of achievement designed to compel students to assimilate knowledge and practice in a particular fashion" (Barbara Finkelstein as quoted in Spring, 2001, p. 144).

Most certainly the scientific movement of the times fortified and supported instructionism as learning results were often quantifiable and measurable. According to Cureton (1971), it was during this time at the turn of the century that many educators were developing their first educational achievement tests in reading, writing, spelling, and arithmetic (p. 6). These tests were built in response to variations in standards and student expectations for learning and were intended to be objective measures of results. Subsequently, in 1914, Frederick J. Kelly created the "multiple choice" testing approach in order to administer tests en masse and eliminate subjectivity of short-answer or essay questions. Society's expectations related to what students should learn (facts) and how they should learn (through memorization) served as a justification for their teacher-centered approach to instruction and assessment. Furthermore, this system of education prepared them for the industrialized economy of the times. Combined with workplace conditions that were not conducive to learner-centered instruction, it was inevitable that instructionism became woven into the fabric of American schooling systems. There were a few teachers, however, who implemented learner-centered strategies in their classrooms despite conditions and cultural norms of the school. In doing so, they typically implemented a mixture or hybrid of learner- and teacher-centered strategies.

The scientific approach to education emerged concurrently with the population growth of US secondary schools. In 1892, the National Education Association (NEA) formed a Committee on Secondary School Studies, often referred to as the "Committee of Ten," for the purpose of addressing the issue of education for secondary students. At that time elementary students had access to a systematic common school, yet secondary education was disorganized and inconsistent across the country, catering to an elite subset of white European American students who were destined for the university. Although the committee recommended 12 years of instruction including 8 years of elementary school followed by 4 of high school for *all* students, it was criticized for its emphasis on preparing a limited number of students for college and not for life or vocation. In response to this criticism, the NEA formed yet another committee called the Commission on the Re-organization of Secondary Education who filed a report in 1918 that put forth "Seven Cardinal Principles" to guide the reorganization of secondary education. Although scholars disagree about the long-term impact of the "Seven Cardinal Principles," many support the claim that these principles perpetuated the factory model of education and further immersed the country into a system of standardization and measurement. The report provided the framework for the organization of the comprehensive high school model, and much of the system remains to this day. Keep in mind, though, that schools were still segregated during this time and would be until 1965.

Modern period (1920–Present). By the mid-1920s, the comprehensive high school model was well established and was intended to accommodate all secondary students regardless of their future into career or college. Enrollment in secondary education grew by leaps and bounds during the next few decades. Curriculum included college preparatory programs of study as well as vocational classes such as bookkeeping, home economics, agriculture, and industry. The comprehensive high school was also intended to "develop democratic ethical sensibilities, civic competencies, and empathy between students from different racial, ethnic, and socioeconomic backgrounds" (Gutek, 1991, p. 110) despite segregation and Jim Crow laws in the South. Criticism of the comprehensive high school grew as some feared that the curriculum was watered down and soft due to the inclusion of vocational courses and a lack of rigor in the intellectual disciplines such as history, mathematics, science, and literature. This concern was exacerbated by the launching of Sputnik in 1957 by the US cold war adversary—the Soviet Union who attributed their success to their superiority in science and mathematics. The 1960s also saw a decline in US SAT scores indicating that students were not academically prepared for college. Great disparity existed among racial and ethnic groups, and social inequities in education continued to rise as US poverty rates rose to approximately 19%. US President Lyndon B. Johnson acknowledged the social inequities and believed that expanding government's role in education had the potential to break the cycle, reduce poverty, and provide equity between the economically disadvantaged and advantaged students.

As a result, the Elementary and Secondary Education Act (ESEA) was passed in 1965 as a part of President Johnson's "War on Poverty" and provided funding, emphasizing equal access to education, and established high standards and accountability. ESEA provided billions of dollars to improve education and expected results in return. The government reauthorized the act every 5 years in a variety of forms with the most recent and noteworthy being No Child Left Behind (NCLB) in 2001 and Every Student Succeeds Act (ESSA) in 2015.

Meanwhile, a minority of teachers implemented learner-centered instruction in elementary schools; however, the dominant pattern of instruction remained teacher centered in most elementary and high schools. Cuban (1993, p. 45) claimed that most teachers found learner-centered practices too time-consuming, too upsetting to existing routines, or too far removed from the conditions they had to face daily (p. 45). Teachers resisted because there were no incentives to make such changes, and they were not sure that the promised outcomes would benefit the children. Therefore, most students were subject to deadening routines, tyrannical authority, and passive learning (Cuban, 1993, p. 151). Teachers continued to rely on the textbook and worked hard to cover the content. Seatwork was common, and teachers used questioning as the primary means of exchanging information and informal assessment, thus perpetuating a wisdom of practice or lore of teaching that anchored instructionism as the accepted approach to teaching. However, during the 1960s, the "informal school" movement gained a modest degree of momentum in a few areas. Informal schools were less structured and were mostly elementary schools that utilized learning centers—tables clustered so that students could collaborate—that increased the use of small groups for instruction and allowed students a bit of freedom to move about the classroom. A very small number of informal schools also allowed students to choose a learning center and decide what to study and how much time to spend on their selected topic. Then in 1970, Jean Piaget released his book *The Science of Education* that helped popularize discovery-based teaching approaches, especially in the sciences, contributing to the knowledge of practice associated with learner-centered teaching.

Unfortunately, although there was a brief nod toward constructivism and learner-centered classrooms in the 1960s in the form of the "informal classroom," and despite the work by Piaget, the 1970s experienced a shift back toward instructionism. In a 1970 Special Message to the Congress of Education Reform, President Richard Nixon asserted that "American education is in urgent need of reform" and claimed that current policies and practices were not working, especially for poor children. He called for "thoughtful redirection to improve our ability to make up for the environmental deficiencies among the poor; for long-range provisions for financial support of schools, for more efficient use of the dollars spent on education; for structural reforms to accommodate new discoveries; and for the enhancement of learning before and beyond the school" (Nixon, 2001). In addition, the business community asserted that financial support for schools should be tied to their productivity, and private firms were often hired to assist schools in raising their achievement scores. A 1975 *Newsweek* article entitled "Why Johnny Can't Write" (Sheils, 1975) fueled the debate about national literacy as the author contended that "Willy-nilly, the U.S. educational system is spawning a generation of semi-literates" and then encouraged a back-to-basics approach to solve the literacy crisis (or "stop the rot" as the author proclaimed)—another step backward, rather than a move toward reform.

THE EMERGENCE OF FORMATIVE ASSESSMENT

As evidenced in the narrative above, prior to the mid-1960s, not much attention had been given to either the nature of learners or learning or what goes on in the classroom related to effective instructional and assessment practices. The focus had been on inputs such as policies, teachers, teacher training, standards, and educational systems as well as outputs like grades and GPAs, graduation rates, SAT and ACT scores, and college or career readiness. However, in 1967, Michael Scriven introduced the notion that evaluations or assessments that occur in the classroom could be used to improve curriculum, not just evaluate programs. He stated:

> [Evaluation] may have a role in the on-going improvement of the curriculum, and with respect to this role several types of questions (goals) may be raised...In another role, the evaluation process may serve to enable administrators to decide whether the entire finished curriculum, refined by use of the evaluation process in its first role, represents a sufficiently significant advance on the available alternatives to justify the expense of adoption by a school system...I propose to use the terms "formative" and "summative" evaluation to qualify evaluation in these roles. (Scriven, 1967, p. 41)

Bloom, Hastings, and Madaus (1971) expanded the use of the terms formative and summative evaluation into what is now considered their generally accepted meanings. Summative evaluations are generally conducted at the end of a unit, semester, or course to determine how much students know for the purpose of grading, certification, evaluation of progress, or for researching the effectiveness of a program or curriculum. Formative evaluations, on the other hand, are those assessments that provided feedback that could lead to corrective behavior during the midst of learning (Box, 2008, p. 15) and are often welcomed by students and teachers because they find them useful in helping them master the material.

In the years that followed, the education world at large began to recognize the importance of formative assessment. By 1989, the American Association for the Advancement of Science (AAAS) released *Science for All Americans* (1989) that promoted the idea that what students learn is influenced by their existing ideas and stressed the importance of informative feedback. The National Research Council (NRC) (1996) encouraged teachers to monitor and adjust instruction on the basis of evidence gained during informal assessment—a hallmark of formative assessment. In addition, the NRC championed self-directed learning for students, encouraging teachers to provide students the opportunity to self-assess and monitor their own progress. Neither entity explicitly used the term "formative assessment," yet the strategies they promoted are components of the processes of formative assessment. The power of formative assessment received limited attention, however, until Paul Black and Dylan Wiliam published *Assessment and Classroom Learning* in 1998 (Box, Dabbs, & Skoog, 2015). Black and Wiliam began by reviewing two critical articles (Crooks, 1988; Natriello, 1987) to serve as a baseline for their study, then subsequently reviewed over 160 journals from several countries during a 9-year period leading to the conclusion that formative assessment was clearly a means to improve student achievement. After that, the educational world, including entities such as the NRC, the Educational Testing Service (ETS), the National Science Teachers Association (NSTA), and the Biological Sciences Curriculum Study (BSCS), began to emphasize its use (Box, 2008, pp. 15–17). For example, an NRC report (2000) emphasized the importance of formative assessment in the science learning environment and cited Black and Wiliam's (1998) research in describing how self-assessment by students and conversations instead of inquisitions were critical attributes of formative assessment. Another NRC report (Bransford, Brown, & Cocking, 2000; National Research

Council, 2005) promoted formative assessment as a key attribute in a learner-centered environment and encouraged its use to support learning. Likewise, other prominent educational entities have initiated reform efforts that support the implementation of formative assessment strategies. For example, the Educational Testing Service in Princeton, NJ, acquired the Assessment Training Institute, whose goal is to provide professional development (PD) programs specifically aimed at improving the use of formative assessment to support student learning. A position paper of the NSTA supported the use of formative assessment and stated "when the outcomes of learning are clearly specified, as they are in the NSES [National Science Education Standards], assessment can and should be used as feedback to improve the learning/teaching process as well as to determine if students are achieving the desired outcomes" (National Science Teachers Association, 2003, par. 11). This position paper cited Black and Wiliam's conclusion that feedback is one of the most effective strategies available to teachers that has the potential to improve student learning. Additionally, the National Academies and the NRC, in their description of educational reform in *Taking Science to School: Learning and Teaching Science in Grades K-8* (2007), revealed formative assessment as one of their major findings and conclusions of research related to student learning. Conclusion 12 stated that:

> Ongoing assessment is an integral part of instruction that can foster student learning when appropriately designed and used regularly. Assessment, whether formative or summative, needs to be responsive to the full range of proficiencies that are implied by the strands. Assessment needs to be aligned with the research on students' thinking as well as informed by the subject matter. (p. 344)

The NRC called for individual teachers, administrators, and school systems to implement well-designed assessments stating that they "can have a tremendous impact on students' learning of science if conducted regularly and used by teachers to alter and improve instruction" (p. 344).

BSCS emphasized formative assessment as an integral part of science education reform in their National Academy for Curriculum Leadership (NACL) PD initiative. The three-year NACL program was created to support school districts who desired to improve their secondary science programs and included the use of formative assessment, among other research-based instructional methods (St. John, Hirabayashi, Helms, & Tambe, 2006).

It is evident that formative assessment has become part of the educational landscape of American systems, and that it is promoted and supported by many reputable educators and educational entities. Yet it arose in a political and socio-cultural environment that has proven unwieldy and very resistant to change.

High-Stakes Testing and the Era of Accountability

As formative assessment gained notice and traction in the educational community, it found itself in tension with the rise of summative, high-stakes testing and an era of accountability. In response to the launching of Sputnik in 1957 and national security concerns, the United States passed the National Defense Education Act (NDEA) of 1958 which is considered one of the first major efforts by the federal government to reform American education. The goal of the legislation was to improve American schools, especially in the areas of science and technology. With it came funding from the Federal treasury for testing at both state and local levels. This landmark legislation expanded the use of educational testing and marked the beginning of large-scale involvement by the US federal government in education.

Moreover, the Civil Rights Act of 1964 called for a survey to document the availability of equal educational opportunities for African American and other minority students as compared to opportunities for white students. Findings were documented in the Equal Educational Opportunity Survey (EEOS), better known as the Coleman Report (Coleman, 1966), and revealed, among other things, that African American children were several grade levels behind their white counterparts in school. This report focused on student achievement scores and changed the way in which we evaluated educational systems and judged the quality of our schools. 1965 saw the passage of the ESEA that provided financial assistance to school districts who served low-income families and to states to help them develop tests. The National Assessment of Educational Progress (NAEP) monitored students at the national level, and although these results were not used to make decisions about individual states or schools, results were often used in calls for reform. The EEOS and ESEA combined to catapult accountability to a new level, resulting in an exponential growth of summative, high-stakes educational testing.

Two significant events further increased the nation's focus on testing in the 1970s: (1) the enactment of the Education for All Handicapped Children Act (EAHCA) of 1975 that mandated all handicapped children have their specific needs identified and met and (2) a decline in SAT scores that alarmed the nation and incited continued debates about the quality of high school education. Oregon was the first state to institute compensatory testing in 1973. Within 6 years, 33 states had some sort of minimum compensatory testing, 18 of which required students to pass tests in order to graduate.

High-stakes testing rose even more after the 1983 publication of *A Nation at Risk* by the National Commission on Excellence in Education. This report revealed that standardized test scores for high school students had dropped in the 26 years since the launching of Sputnik, and called for serious reform of American educational systems.

In 1989, a coalition of state governors along with President George H.W. Bush met together to lay the groundwork for Goals 2000: Educate America Act that established eight goals for American education. On March 26, 1994, under President Bill Clinton, the act was passed by the US Congress. The bill was intended to "improve learning and teaching by providing a national framework for education reform; to promote the research, consensus building, and systemic changes needed to ensure equitable educational opportunities and high levels of educational achievement for all American students" (Congress, 1994). The competencies therein identified what students should know and be able to do in the twenty-first century, and in order to help authorities determine if those goals were being met, high-stakes tests were administered. Those high-stakes test then had a strong influence on instructional decisions. "Once high stakes tests are put into place, they become the de facto standards. For teachers, the content of the tests define what they teach" (Madaus et al., 2009, p. 20). None of the goals established were ever reached, but testing was once again promoted as the policy tool of choice to hold schools and individuals accountable. In 1997, the Individuals with Disabilities Education Act or IDEA was enacted and further contributed to the testing movement. This act called for accountability measures for the 5.8 million children with disabilities in an effort to ensure that all students received equal and fair education.

On January 8, 2002, in the wake of the standards-and-testing movement that ensued after *A Nation at Risk* was published, President George W. Bush reauthorized ESEA as the NCLB Act. NCLB provided federal resources to states to improve low-performing schools and was intended to close the achievement gap with accountability, flexibility, and choice. The Act called for greater accountability which led to a sharp increase in standardized testing in most states (Black & Wiliam, 2005; Box, 2008; Chappuis & Chappuis, 2007; Nichols & Berliner, 2008). The ESSA, signed into law in December 2015 by President Barack Obama, is the latest reauthorization of ESEA at the time of this writing and shifted responsibility from federal to expanded state control. States are still required to administer annual tests in reading and math in grades 3–8 and once in high school, but how test results are used is now a state and local matter.

Consequences of high-stakes testing. Although there are a host of deleterious effects on education attributed to high-stakes testing, we will focus on how testing has affected the classroom practices related to the process of learning. Instructionism, the ineffective yet well-established mode of instruction, saw an encouraging decline shortly after the release of *How People Learn: Brain, Mind, Experience, and School* (HPL) (Bransford et al., 2000). This seminal work published in 2000 by the NRC provided significant findings about how students learn and linked those findings to practice. Prior to its release, most educators continued to operate under behaviorist theories that viewed learning as a process of forming connections between stimuli and response and a reliance upon the measurement of observable data. Behaviorism neglected the inner mental processes related to learning as they were considered elusive and subjective. Thus, educators subscribed to established norms of instructionism, believing that students learned through listening to their teacher, memorization, and drill and practice, and learning was evidenced through recitation of declarative knowledge. However, in the 1970s, a technological revolution ensued, and new experimental tools and methodologies made it possible for scientists to actually test their theories about learning: giving birth to the new field of cognitive science. The cognitive sciences included knowledge drawn from neuroscience, anthropology, linguistics, philosophy, developmental psychology, computer sciences, and socio-cognitive studies. The cognitive sciences combined knowledge base is referred to as the *learning sciences* or the *science of learning*. Their findings revolutionized what we know about the processes of the mind during learning. However, this potential paradigm shift occurred at the peak of high-stakes testing, which created a significant tug-of-war between a teacher's desire for students to score well on the test and the desire to provide quality instruction that leads to deep learning. The paradox here is that while educators are encouraged to teach through learner-centered practices that lead to deep understanding, we continue to test declarative knowledge that can often be conquered by memorization and time-honored practices of instructionism. In addition, we have found that when the stakes are high, teachers and students do not worry about the niceties of a well-rounded education. The standardized test is portrayed as the common enemy, and any strategy used by teachers or students to cope with it is justified (Madaus et al., 2009, p. 143).

Although some studies suggested that high-stakes testing has little influence over pedagogy (Gradwell, 2006; Hillocks, 2002; van Hover & Pierce, 2006; Yeh, 2005), there is a preponderance of evidence that it does. Wayne Au (2011) claimed that US public schools have returned to the days of Taylorism as teachers' classroom practices are increasingly standardized by high-stakes testing and scripted curriculum (p. 25). In a meta-synthesis of 49 qualitative studies, Au (2007) found a significant relationship between the implementation of high-stakes testing and changes in the types of pedagogy associated with teaching the content. "A significant number of participants in qualitative studies reported that their pedagogy changed in response to high-stakes tests and that a significant majority of the changes included an increase in teacher-centered instruction associated with lecturing and the direct transmission of test-related facts" (Au, 2007, p. 263). Au did find a small number of teachers who increased their use of learner-centered practices, but they were the exception, rather than the rule. Blazar and Pollard (2017) conducted a study to determine if quality of instruction differed between teachers and classrooms with varying levels of engagement in test preparation. They concluded that test preparation was "a significant and negative predictor of the ambitious and inquiry-oriented nature of upper elementary teachers' mathematics instruction" (p. 428), congruent with other research findings (Amrein & Berliner, 2002; Diamond, 2007; Koretz, 2005; Madaus et al., 2009; Wright, 2002), that described a decline in quality instruction and an unfortunate reversion to instructionist pedagogy (Sawyer, 2014, p. 729).

To complicate matters further, high-stakes testing has the potential to create competition among schools, teachers, and students with an emphasis on grades instead of learning. It often results in teaching a restricted curriculum with a focus on declarative knowledge and test-taking strategies and skills, replacing high-quality forms of instruction. Teaching under these conditions often leads to teaching for breadth not depth as teachers try to cover all of the required competencies, and in many cases, the focus tends to be on "bubble kids" or those who need to improve their scores and close achievement gaps, often to the detriment of other students.

Where We Stand: Student Achievement

Despite efforts at reform, a recent study by Harvard's Program on Education Policy and Governance and Education Next (Hanushek, Peterson, & Woessmann, 2012) asserted that learning gains have been marginal since 1995. Hanushek, et al. (2012) analyzed fourth and eighth graders' growth in math, science, and reading scores from one US series of tests and three tests administered by international organizations and found that while 24 countries trail the US rate of improvement, another 24 countries appear to be improving at a faster rate, putting us squarely in the middle of developed and newly developing parts of the world. There have been a few bright spots, however. For example, US students in elementary schools do seem to be performing considerably better than they were a couple of decades ago. Most notably, the performance of 4th grade students on math tests rose steeply between the mid-1990s and 2011. However, the current rate of improvement overall is not sufficiently rapid enough to allow the United States to catch up with leaders of the industrialized world. Hanushek et al. also claimed that:

> States who have shown the most improvement are those who have embraced reform. There is some hint that those parts of the United States that took school reform the most seriously—Florida and North Carolina, for example—have shown stronger rates of improvement, while states that have steadfastly resisted many school reforms (Iowa and Wisconsin, for instance) are among the nation's test-score laggards. But the connection between reforms and gains adduced thus far is only anecdotal, not definitive. (p. 17)

Although it is common to track and analyze achievement scores, the results only provide evidence of knowledge and skills in specific content areas, neglecting aptitudes and dispositions that are historically difficult to measure. In a knowledge economy that relies on higher level thinking such as the collection, analysis, and synthesis of information, achievement tests in content areas may fall short of providing the information that we need to determine if our students are ready to face twenty-first-century challenges. It would be wise to respond to US student achievement results on tests such as the Programme for International Student Assessment (PISA) that are designed to measure a students' ability to apply knowledge and skills in key subject areas as well as their ability to analyze, reason, and communicate effectively as they pose, interpret, and solve problems (National Research Council, 2013, p. 15). Results for American students have been mediocre thus far and should serve as an indicator of what needs to change in our system. Primarily, our students need to be equipped with the tools required to think critically and regulate their own learning, a primary aim of formative assessment.

CONCLUSION

It is clear that the United States, despite its good intentions, is still entrenched in a system that was formed out of dire necessity to educate the masses and that we have yet to break free from the structures that constrain us, although there are glimpses of hope and progress. The following chapter delves into the positive effects of formative assessment on student agency and achievement, the potential that it has to transform learning, and discusses the learning environment that it requires in order to flourish.

WORKS CITED

66 Special Message to the Congress on Education Reform. March 3, 1970. (2001). *American Reference Library – Primary Source Documents*, 1.
American Association for the Advancement of Science. (1989). *Science for all Americans*. New York: Oxford University Press.
Amrein, A. L., & Berliner, D. C. (2002). High-stakes testing and student learning. *Education Policy Analysis Archives, 10*, 18.
Au, W. (2007). High-stakes testing and curricular control: A qualitative metasynthesis. *Educational Researcher, 36*(5), 258–267.
Au, W. (2011). Teaching under the new Taylorism: High-stakes testing and the standardization of the 21st century curriculum. *Journal of Curriculum Studies, 43*(1), 25–45.
Black, P., & Wiliam, D. (1998). *Inside the black box: Raising standards through classroom assessment*. London: nferNelson Publishing Company.
Black, P., & Wiliam, D. (2005). Lessons from around the world: How policies, politics and cultures constrain and afford assessment practices. *Curriculum Journal, 16*(2), 249–261.
Blazar, D., & Pollard, C. (2017). Does test preparation mean low-quality instruction? *Educational Researcher, 46*(8), 420–433.
Bloom, B. S., Hastings, J. T., & Madaus, G. F. (1971). *Handbook of formative and summative evaluation of student learning*. New York: McGraw-Hill.
Box, C., Dabbs, J., & Skoog, G. (2015). A case study of teacher personal practice assessment theories and complexities of implementing formative assessment. *American Educational Research Journal – Teaching, Learning and Human Development, 52*(5), 956–983.

Box, M. C. (2008). *Formative assessment: Patterns, personal practice assessment theories, and impact on student achievement and motivation in science* (PhD dissertation), Texas Tech University, Lubbock, TX.

Bransford, J. D., Brown, A. L., & Cocking, R. R. (Eds.). (2000). *How people learn: Brain, mind, experience, and school.* Washington, DC: National Academy Press.

Chappuis, S., & Chappuis, J. (2007). The best value in formative assessment. *Educational Leadership, 65*(4), 14–19.

Coleman, J. S. (1966). *Equality of educational opportunity.* Washington, DC: U.S. Department of Health, Education, and Welfare; Office of Education.

Crooks, T. J. (1988). The impact of classroom evaluation practices on students. *Review of Educational Research, 58*(4), 438–481.

Cuban, L. (1993). *How teachers taught: Constancy and change in American classrooms, 1890–1990* (2nd ed.). New York: Teachers College Press.

Cureton, L. W. (1971). The history of grading practices. *National Council on Measurement in Education, 2*(4), 1–9.

Diamond, J. B. (2007). Where the rubber meets the road: Rethinking the connection between high-stakes testing policy and classroom instruction. *Sociology of Education, 80*(4), 285–313.

Drury, D., & Baer, J. (2011). *The American public school teacher: Past, present, and future.* Cambridge, MA: Harvard Education Press.

Gradwell, J. M. (2006). Teaching in spite of, rather than because of, the test: A case of ambitious history teaching in New York State. In S. G. Grant (Ed.), *Measuring history: Cases of state-level testing across the United States. Research in curriculum and instruction* (pp. 157–176). Greenwich, CT: Information Age Publishing, Inc.

Gutek, G. L. (1991). *An historical introduction to American education* (2nd ed.). Prospect Heights, IL: Waveland Press.

Hanushek, E. A., Peterson, P. E., & Woessmann, L. (2012). *Achievement growth: International and U.S. state trends in student performance. PEPG Report No.: 12–03.* Retrieved from https://eric.ed.gov/?id=ED534652

Hassenpflug, A., & Hassenpflug. (2010). Harris, William Torrey (1835–1909). In T. C. Hunt, J. C. Carper & T. J. Lasley (Ed.), *Encyclopedia of educational reform and dissent.* Thousand Oaks, CA: Sage Publications. Retrieved from http://search.credoreference.com/content/entry/sageerd/harris_william_torrey_1835_1909/0

Hillocks, G. (2002). *The testing trap: How state writing assessments control learning.* New York: Teachers College Press.

van Hover, S., & Pierce, E. (2006). "Next year will be different:" Two first-year history teachers' perceptions of the impact of Virginia's accountability reform on their instructional decision-making. *Journal of Social Studies Research, 30*(2), 38–50.

Koretz, D. (2005). *Alignment, high stakes, and the inflation of test scores. CSE report 655*. California University, Los Angeles Center for the Study of Evaluation. Retrieved from https://eric.ed.gov/?id=ED488711

Labaree, D. F. (2005). Progressivism, schools and schools of education: An American romance. *Paedagogica Historica: International Journal of the History of Education, 41*(1–2), 275–288.

Leidecker, K. F. (1946). *Yankee teacher: The life of William Torrey Harris*. New York: The Philosophical Library.

Madaus, G. F., Russell, M. K., & Higgins, J. (2009). *The paradoxes of high stakes testing: How they affect students, their parents, teachers, principals, schools, and society*. Charlotte, NC: Information Age Publishing.

National Research Council. (1996). *National science education standards*. Washington, DC: National Academy Press.

National Research Council. (2000). *Inquiry and the national science education standards*. Washington, DC: National Academies Press.

National Research Council. (2005). *How students learn science in the classroom*. Washington, DC: The National Academies Press.

National Research Council. (2007). *Taking science to school: Learning and teaching science in grades K-8*. Washington, DC: The National Academies Press.

National Research Council. (2013). *Education for life and work: Developing transferable knowledge and skills in the 21st century*. Washington, DC: The National Academies Press.

National Science Teachers Association. (2003). *NSTA position statement beyond 2000 – Teachers of science speak out*. Retrieved from http://www.nsta.org/about/positions/beyond2000.aspx

Natriello, G. (1987). The impact of evaluation processes on students. *Educational Psychologist, 21*(2), 155.

Nichols, S. L., & Berliner, D. C. (2008). Testing the joy out of learning. *Educational Leadership, 65*(6), 14–18.

Nixon, R. (2001). 66 Special Message to the Congress on Education Reform. March 3, 1970. *American Reference Library – Primary Source Documents*, 1.

Papert, S. (1993). *The children's machine: Rethinking school in the age of the computer*. New York: BasicBooks.

Public Law 103-227. (1994). Goals 2000: Educate America Act, 103-227 C.F.R.

Sawyer, R. K. (2014). Conclusion: The future of learning: Grounding educational innovation in the learning sciences. In R. K. Sawyer (Ed.), *The Cambridge handbook of the learning sciences* (2nd ed., pp. 726–746). New York, NY: Cambridge University Press.

Scriven, M. (1967). Perspectives of curriculum evaluation. In R. W. Tyler, R. M. Gagne, & M. Scriven (Eds.), *The methodology of evaluation* (pp. 39–83). Chicago: Rand McNally.

Sheils, M. (1975). Why Johnny can't write. *Newsweek*, December 8.

Spring, J. H. (2001). *The American school, 1642–2000* (5th ed.). Boston: McGraw-Hill.

St. John, M., Hirabayashi, J., Helms, J. V., & Tambe, P. (2006). *The BSCS National Academy for Curriculum Leadership: Contributions and lessons learned. An evaluation brief.* Inverness Research Associates.

Thorndike, E. L. (1904). *Theory of mental and social measurements.* New York: The Science Press.

Wright, W. E. (2002). The effects of high stakes testing in an inner-city elementary school: The curriculum, the teachers, and the English language learners. *Current Issues in Education, 5.*

Yeh, S. S. (2005). Limiting the unintended consequences of high-stakes testing. *Education Policy Analysis Archives, 13,* 43.

CHAPTER 2

The Power of Formative Assessment

Formative assessment has become part of the educational landscape in the United States and is heralded to be an important tool for success, yet we are often uncertain what it is and what it looks like in the classroom. This chapter will clarify the purpose and meaning of formative assessment and will explain the importance of an environment that facilitates effective implementation. In addition, it will provide a survey of the research and highlight the substantial body of evidence that supports its use as well as problems educators have encountered translating theory into practice.

Formative Assessment

Although formative assessment or Assessment *for* Learning (A*f*L) has been part of the educational landscape now for many years, there is still no single definition for the practice and the term. Some authors have described it as:

> All those activities undertaken by teachers, and by their students in assessing themselves, which provide information to be used as feedback to modify the teaching and learning activities in which they are engaged. Such assessment becomes 'formative assessment' when the evidence is actually used to adapt the teaching work to meet the needs. (Black & Wiliam, 1998b, p. 2)

> In Assessments *for* Learning, the assessment purpose is to provide teachers and students with information they need along the way, during the learning process, to make decisions that will bring about more learning. (Stiggins & Chappuis, 2005, p. 17)

> Formative assessment is a planned process in which assessment-elicited evidence of students' status is used by teachers to adjust their ongoing instructional procedures or by students to adjust their current learning tactics. (Popham, 2008)
>
> Assessment *for* Learning is part of everyday practice by students, teachers and peers that seeks, reflects upon and responds to information from dialogue, demonstration and observation in ways that enhance ongoing learning. (Klenowski, 2009, p. 264)
>
> Formal and informal processes teachers and students use to gather evidence for the purpose of improving learning. (Chappuis, 2015)

In order to clarify and refine, several entities engaged in a concerted effort to establish a clearer description of formative assessment and its guiding principles. Most notably, the Council of Chief State School Officers' (CCSSO) Formative Assessment for Students and Teachers (FAST) State Collaborative on Assessment and Student Standards (SCASS) developed this definition of formative assessment that sums it up very clearly:

> Formative assessment is a process used by teachers and students during instruction that provides feedback to adjust ongoing teaching and learning to improve students' achievement of intended instructional outcomes. (McManus, 2008)

Note from these descriptions that formative assessment focuses on improving student learning rather than on the evaluation of what they have already learned, hence the oft-used alternative term, Assessment *for* Learning, that lies in contrast to summative evaluations or Assessment *of* Learning. The processes of formative assessment cross traditional boundaries, involving both the teacher *and* the student, and evidence from the assessment has a direct impact on what comes next in the learning process. Thus, it is important that the teacher designs and implements learning events that result in timely and accurate evidence that is informative and directly related to the desired learning outcomes so that adjustments can be made. Flexibility and responsiveness on both the part of the teacher to adjust instruction and the part of the student to monitor and adjust his/her learning techniques are essential.

The ultimate aim of formative assessment, in addition to making teachers more effective, is to equip and empower students to become self-regulated, life-long learners in an environment that deepens the learning, as students think critically about the content and about their own cognition. The role of the student as partner clearly distinguishes formative assessment from most other types of traditional assessments wherein the teacher is the primary assessor and takes sole responsibility to determine where students are in the learning process and what needs to change. This normative behavior by teachers is deeply rooted and culturally entrenched, and as a result, many teachers find themselves reluctant to provide opportunities for students to self-assess. Reasons for this reluctance are abundant and complex but may boil down to a misplaced sense of responsibility related to educational goals, a lack of trust in students, a lack of knowledge and pedagogical skills needed to effectively involve students, or simply, a tendency to adhere to tradition. Unfortunately, many teachers believe their primary responsibility is to produce high achievers rather than life-long learners, and this belief creates a heightened need for control of student learning. When the aim is high achievement, teachers tend to rely on a repertoire of strategies or gimmicks directed toward improving scores rather than implementing strategies that focus on or include student-directed learning opportunities. In addition, some teachers may harbor a skeptical, negative view of students and their motivation, not trusting them to accurately or effectively monitor their own learning. To illustrate, during an interview with a traditional, instructivist teacher early in my research career, she claimed that it was too difficult to give students any measure of control. She maintained that students were generally apathetic and not inclined to put forth the effort necessary for them to construct knowledge. When asked about putting the learning into the hands of her students, she stated:

> I would love to be able to start off the school year with just a simple little problem and get the kids in groups and say, I need you to figure out how to solve this. And let the kids start brainstorming. But once again, the kids are like, 'oh god if it takes much effort', they are like 'I don't want to do this, this is too hard', they'll say. (Box, 2008, p. 159)

This teacher's distrust of students and their motivation or work ethic prevented her from shifting the responsibility to them—the stakes were too high. Other reasons that may prevent teachers from relinquishing control include a lack of adequate training (to be discussed in Chap. 5) or simply a dominant folk pedagogy that is counter-cultural to practices that purposefully promote student ownership, rendering some teachers unable or unwilling to venture out or "swim upstream" as it were.

Equipping and Empowering Students

There are practical ways that teachers can purposefully empower students in their own learning, if they are willing to share the responsibility. Nilson's book, *Creating Self-Regulated Learners (2013)*, distinguished the difference between self-regulated learning and metacognition asserting that self-regulation is the more general concept, and metacognition is a major facet of self-regulation. Thus, metacognition is the control over one's own cognitive processes, while self-regulation encompasses the monitoring and managing of one's cognitive processes as well as the "awareness of and control over one's emotions, motivations, behavior, and environment as related to learning" (p. 5). For our purposes, this narrative will focus on metacognitive strategies that contribute to self-regulatory behaviors as encompassed in the processes of formative assessment as described by experts such as Black, Harrison, Lee, Marshall, and Wiliam (2002), Schraw and Dennison (1994), Lamar and Lodge (2014), Zimmerman (2002), Locke and Latham (2006), Latham and Brown (2006), Tanner (2012), Nilson (2013), Chappuis (2015), and McGuire (2015). The important point here is that these skills can be taught during guided instruction as teachers provide students the opportunity to monitor and control their learning.

Before instruction. At the beginning of the academic year, as the teacher sets the stage for empowering students in their own learning, it is beneficial to partner with students in this endeavor and have them begin to consider the power of metacognition. This outcome may be accomplished through the use of a variety of instruments such as the Metacognitive Awareness Inventory (MAI) (Mytkowicz, Goss, & Steinberg, 2014; Young & Fry, 2008) that is used by students to assess their perceptions about their own development of declarative, procedural, and conditional knowledge as well as their self-awareness of learning, planning strategies, and implementation, monitoring, and evaluation of learning strategies. This process helps the student become aware of their regulatory strengths and weaknesses and can guide the teacher as they decide what strategies need the most work. It can be re-administered at the end of the year to help students become aware of their growth in the continual cycle of building awareness and metacognitive competency.

In order for students to regulate their own learning, they need to know what the learning goals are and what success looks like. Often this is accomplished by rewriting the competencies into student friendly terms, sharing them with the students, and referring to them often. However, if students are to truly partner with the teacher to construct their own knowledge, then they should have a clear understanding of the rationale for existing criteria, plus have a say in what constitutes mastery. In addition, the instructional models and learning strategies that teachers design and implement must result in frequent and reliable evidence that can be used to determine where students are in the learning process. In other words, learning must be visible in some form or fashion.

It is also beneficial at the beginning of a unit to ask students to assess their pre-existing knowledge or level of skill related to the content to be studied. Learning improves when students spend time thinking about what they already know, what they might not know, and what they think can be learned before beginning a unit of study. This can be accomplished through knowledge surveys, or some type of traffic light activity. Traffic lighting calls for students to signify their degree of confidence or categorize their understanding using green, yellow, or red according to whether they think they have good, partial, or little understanding of the concept at hand. These labels serve as a simple means for students to communicate their perceived levels of understanding. It also makes the learning targets very clear to students before they begin the unit of study.

During instruction. Teachers should (1) activate students as resources for one another through the provision of collaborative activities, (2) provide timely and effective feedback that students can use to adjust their teaching tactics, and (3) equip and empower students as they self-assess and set goals.

Collaboration. At this juncture, it is important to distinguish between traditional group work and true collaboration. Students who work in pairs or groups are not necessarily collaborating and serving as resources for one another. Collaboration is defined as the process of building and maintaining a shared conception of a problem or task, distributing responsibility across members of the group, sharing expertise, and mutually constructing and negotiating cognition (Roschelle, 1992). True collaboration occurs when students work within their respective zones of proximal development to lend their unique perspective to the group, each student having varying levels of knowledge and skills from which to draw. Students grow as they work collaboratively through their task to attain a mutually shared cognition, being held accountable and serving as resources for one another. This approach contrasts with group work where students may "divide and conquer" in order to get the job done—an emphasis on performance, rather than learning.

Feedback. Many research studies have produced clear and convincing evidence that feedback is vitally important in the learning process and, if executed appropriately, has the potential to significantly improve achievement. Conversely, if feedback is incorrectly proffered or neglected all together it can be detrimental to learning. In a nutshell, effective feedback helps students know where they are in the learning process and points them in the right direction when needed. It is important that the feedback is given early while there is time for a student to use it and act on it. However, the nature and amount of feedback is important as well—not too much and not too little. Furthermore, the feedback does not do the thinking for the student, but rather helps the students in the process of finding solutions or answers (Chappuis, 2015). Thus, feedback may be directed toward metacognitive processes, skills, and related content as appropriate.

Self-assess and set goals. Once the curricular learning targets have been clarified, the teacher should guide students to assess their individual progress toward achieving the learning targets and set personal goals accordingly. The teacher should provide opportunities for students to reflect periodically about both the process and their progress. As the classroom teacher mentors students through the process, self-reflection has the potential to deepen the learning and puts the student squarely in the driver's seat. It can increase motivation when there is clear evidence of progress or help students redirect their efforts when progress lags. *The Cambridge Handbook of the Learning Sciences* (Sawyer, 2014, p. 3) claimed that students learn better when they express their developing knowledge and then analyze their state of knowledge. Students can use learning logs, evidence portfolios, tracking forms, conversations, reports, or other platforms to monitor their growth throughout the learning cycle.

Goal setting strategies are important for students as they develop the ability to reflect on their learning and assess progress. Often, students tend to set performance goals rather than learning goals, thus the habit of focusing on *learning* must be instilled and fostered. Mastery or learning goals are more effective at helping students grow and monitor their own progress, resulting in higher levels of engagement and satisfaction in students' academic progress. Repeating this process throughout a course allows students to practice self-assessment and identify areas of weakness and strength. Additionally, students should contemplate their selection of study strategies and corresponding levels of success. Did the approach work? What evidence supports it? What are potential alternative strategies? Students should engage in PCI to improve their learning behaviors in the same manner that teachers do to improve their teaching.

At the end of instruction. At the end of an instructional unit, the teacher should provide students the opportunity to show evidence of mastery and use the evidence to revise their goals as necessary. A powerful strategy that directs students to monitor their learning and set revised goals is often referred to as a "test autopsy." While taking a test, students indicate their level of confidence in each answer, then after the test is graded and returned, they analyze each wrong answer. For each wrong answer, they indicate whether they missed it due to a simple mistake, or a lack of knowledge or understanding. Additionally, students are asked to examine their study habits in a post-test analysis. This post-test analysis prompts students to think about their own learning, including study strategies, and determine what works and what does not. It is important that along with reflection students set concrete learning goals for improvement as they seek to find ways to close the learning gaps. Some questions on the test autopsy might include "What study strategies did you use to prepare for this exam?," "How happy are you with the results of the exam?," "Did you know the information that you needed to know in order to be successful?," "What percentage of questions did you miss due to simple mistakes?," "What percentage did you miss due to complete lack of understanding?," and "What stumps you?" Using this analytic approach after each test enhances students' awareness and regulation of cognition.

Lastly, throughout the learning process, students should be given the opportunity to share their progress through evidence portfolios, journals, or learning logs. "Knowing you have made progress toward a goal reinforces the value of effort. Incremental success leads to incremental growth in students' confidence in their capabilities as learners, which promotes greater effort, which in turn leads to higher achievement" (Chappuis, 2015, p. 269).

A Portrait of Formative Assessment in Practice

The previous section briefly described ways to empower and equip students, a primary aim of formative assessment. A bridge metaphor introduced by Marie Furtak (2005) helps further conceptualize the role that assessment can play in helping students achieve their learning goals (Box, 2008). In this metaphor, one side of the gap represents the current place where students sit (Point A) and the other represents student learning goals and what success looks like (Point B), and the distance between the two comprises a gap that needs to be bridged (see Fig. 2.1). It is important to point out that the gap described when discussing formative assessment is the lack of student knowledge or skill relative to the identified learning target. It is

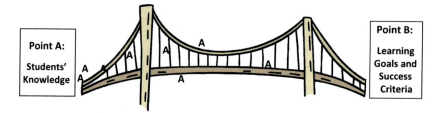

Fig. 2.1 A visual representation of the learning bridge as described by Furtak (2005)

not the "gap" commonly described when teachers analyze summative data and observe deficiencies in student learning. Teachers and students alike should be cognizant of where each student's "Point A" is when instruction begins and at critical points throughout the learning progression. In order to establish the magnitude of the gap, the teacher must orchestrate activities that elicit enough evidence to make the students' thinking visible so that their levels of understanding can be compared to the goal—"Point B." "While the gap metaphor lacks the complexity inherent in any classroom activity, it does capture the possibility of how assessment can provide teachers and students with information that can inform actions that bridge the gap" (Furtak, 2005, p. 6).

So what might formative assessment look like in practice? To set the stage and provide an environment that is conducive to continual growth, teachers create an emotionally safe, risk-tolerant community of learners where mistakes are expected and used to improve learning. Teachers design learning frameworks that support the construction of knowledge related to the learning targets and plan and implement effective collaborative learning and assessment activities. They support students as they think critically about the content and encourage divergent thinking and lively discourse by students as they learn and grow.

In a classroom that effectively implements formative assessment, learning targets and success criteria (Point B) are very clear. Teachers work with their colleagues to unpack the standards and determine what students should know and be able to do and what mastery looks like. They ensure that students know what the learning targets are and share with them the attributes of quality work. Teachers also provide the rationale for criteria, allowing students to contribute based on their own judgments and experiences. There are no surprises or mysteries related to expectations for learning.

Evidence of student mastery is used by both the teacher and the student to determine next steps in the process. Teachers provide effective and timely feedback to move the learning forward. Throughout the process, students use both the teacher and their fellow students as a resource and actively participate in learning activities as they strive to close learning gaps. They set learning goals and partner with the teacher and their fellow students in determining where they are on the learning continuum (Point A) through self and peer assessments and reflection, as well as from teacher feedback, keeping track of their own progress. Teachers use the evidence of mastery to determine curricular changes that need to be made and students use the evidence to adjust their own study skills, habits, and strategies, utilizing and strengthening their metacognitive skills in the process. Grades are based on mastery as both teachers and students monitor their progress toward the learning goals.

It is evident from this description that the process of formative assessment is not something to be layered on top of an already bulging curriculum and disparate set of instructional strategies but is rather meant to be the norm—replacing instructivistic habits and ineffective traditions of the classroom. It calls for a structural framework that is learner-centered, that enables, supports, and measures the incremental growth of students throughout the learning process.

Getting started. The very idea of such a significant shift in practice may sound daunting, but is possible, and starts with wise and proper planning. The use of Wiggins and McTighe's backward design serves as a useful framework for planning the learning experiences—it begins with the end in mind, considering what success looks like and what would potentially constitute evidence of success, before planning the learning activities. This approach to planning assures that one focuses on intended outcomes, rather than on content or curriculum, and ensures that the activities align with the learning targets. Once the learning targets, success criteria, and potential evidence of success have been set, there are many different models of instruction that are constructivist and if implemented with integrity promote student empowerment, such as the 5E Learning Cycle, problem-based learning, inquiry-based learning, discovery learning, experiential learning, and flipped learning to name a few. Keep in mind that in constructivism, students create meaning in their own mind and the designer of the curriculum should provide opportunities that allow them opportunities to do so. Additionally, evidence of success produced by students should not be too prescriptive and overly structured but should allow and encourage creativity and individuality.

As the curriculum designer plans learning activities associated with the construction of knowledge, they should intentionally embed assessment practices along the way. It just makes sense that as students create meaning, they should be prompted to monitor and regulate their learning as they go. Assessment should not be an afterthought or left to chance, but rather be a planned, integral part of the curriculum. Jan Chappuis (2015) in her book *Seven Strategies of Assessment for Learning* provided a logical way to embed the processes of formative assessment within the curricular design. This structure has the potential to help teachers and students develop the repertoire of practices needed to effectively implement formative assessment strategies into their learning frameworks. The seven strategies proposed by Chappuis are formulated around three essential questions: (1) Where am I going? (2) Where am I now?, and (3) How can I close the gap? These strategies are designed to be seamlessly adapted into existing curriculum.

Where Am I Going?

Strategy 1: Provide students with a clear and understandable vision of the learning target.
Strategy 2: Use examples and models of strong and weak work.

Where Am I Now?

Strategy 3: Offer regular descriptive feedback during the learning.
Strategy 4: Teach students to self-assess and set goals for next steps.

How Can I Close the Gap?

Strategy 5: Use evidence of student learning needs to determine next steps in teaching.
Strategy 6: Design focused instruction, followed by practice with feedback.
Strategy 7: Provide students opportunities to track, reflect on, and share their learning progress.

Each strategy within the model is congruent with the tenets of formative assessment as they put students squarely in the driver's seat, empowering them as self-regulated learners. Notice that each essential question is written from the students' perspective. Ongoing feedback and self-assessments create opportunities for deeper learning as they partner with "more knowledgeable others" such as their teacher and fellow students.

This model provides concrete strategies that can be implemented throughout a unit of learning that carries the process through a natural progression from the very beginning of a lesson to closing the learning gap at the end, and it provides a recursive loop when necessary. It also empowers students to take an active role in their learning:

> The seven strategies described here are designed to help students better understand their learning goals, recognize their own skill level in relation to the goals, and take responsibility for reaching the goals. By expanding our formative assessment practices to systematically involve students as decision makers, teachers acknowledge the contributions that students make to their own success and give them the opportunity and structure they need to become active partners in improving their learning. (Chappuis, 2005)

There are other reliable models as well. For example, Dylan Wiliam, in *Embedded Formative Assessment* (2011), made the case for five key strategies, also divided into three categories including (1) Where the learner is going, (2) Where the learner is now, and (3) How to get there. These strategies include:

1. Clarifying, sharing, and understanding learning intentions and criteria for success
2. Engineering effective classroom discussions, activities, and learning tasks that elicit evidence of learning
3. Providing feedback that moves the learning forward
4. Activating learners as instructional resources for one another
5. Activating learners as the owners of their own learning.

This model directly addresses the need for instruction that is more learner-centered as it calls for activities and tasks that elicit evidence of learning and calls for a community of learners as students are empowered to monitor their own progress and to help each other along the way.

As you can see, the traditional, teacher-centered classroom that relies on instructionism sits in sharp contrast to the learning frameworks required to incorporate the processes of formative assessment. Traditional instruction positions the student as passive recipients, and explicit evidence of learning is notably absent as they sit quietly in their desks, taking notes and preparing for exams. A classroom that implements effective processes of formative assessment clearly calls for a learner-centered environment.

Formative Assessment and Effective Learning Environments

As mentioned in Chap. 1, we know that through the twentieth century educators continued to rely on behaviorism to guide their teaching, or they simply succumbed to tradition and cultural norms of the school and taught in a fashion similar to their colleagues, giving little thought, if any, to the theory behind their actions. The goal for students was compliance and memorization, rather than empowerment and critical thinking. Assessments tended to be summative in the form of quizzes or tests and had little bearing on what came next in instruction, much less included the student as decision maker.

In the early 1960s, Russian psychologist Lev Vygotsky's work set the stage for constructivism by asserting three themes describing the role of social interaction, the effect of the more knowledgeable other, and the idea of a zone of proximal development (ZPD). Vygotsky asserted that social interaction plays a major role in the processes of cognitive development, instead of viewing learning as an independent process. When students interact with "the more knowledgeable other," such as the teacher, coach, a peer, or a computer, they are more likely to develop higher level thinking skills as they work through their ZPD. The ZPD is the distance between the student's ability to perform a task under adult guidance and/or with peer collaboration and the student's ability to solve problems independently. According to Vygotsky, learning occurs in this zone. His theory promoted learning contexts in which students collaborate and play an active role in their own construction of knowledge, very different from the teacher-centered, instructivist, transmission model of learning.

Since that time, constructivist theories of learning have been widely accepted by most educators and provide a clearer picture of how students learn. Social constructivism posits that learning is an active, constructive process in which students create their own representations through experiences and that learning is shaped by their prior knowledge, skills, beliefs, and understandings. They learn by doing—not simply listening or observing.

The science of learning. Concurrent with the emergence of constructivism in the 1970s, a technological revolution ensued, and new experimental tools and methodologies were developed that made it possible for scientists to actually test their theories about learning. By the turn of the twenty-first century, scientists were able to conduct electrophysiological studies and neuropsychological tests in addition to neuroimaging techniques that illuminated the complex network between neurons and how they change during learning.

Consequently, research has revealed that the brain is much more malleable than previously believed and that its structure and function can change in response to experiences, even in older brains. Although the findings related to neuroplasticity and its impact on educational practice are numerous (and outside the scope of this writing), there is still much to be discovered about how the brain organizes itself to retain and retrieve knowledge. These findings have great implications for teaching, learning and development, and will for years to come (Draganski et al., 2004; Fitzgerald & Laurian-Fitzgerald, 2016; Gülpinar, 2005; Ludvik, 2016; Maguire, Woollett, & Spiers, 2006; Sousa, 2006; Tovar-Moll & Lent, 2016).

It is evident that findings in the neurosciences clearly validate the tenets of constructivism, revealing the flaws in the instructivist approach to teaching and learning. Consider the key findings released in *How People Learn* (Bransford, Brown, & Cocking, 2000, pp. 14–19). They stated that:

1. Students come to the classroom with preconceptions about how the world works. If their initial understanding is not engaged, they may fail to grasp the new concepts and information that are taught, or they may learn them for purposes of a test but revert to their preconceptions outside the classroom.
2. To develop competence in an area of inquiry, students must (1) have a deep foundation of factual knowledge, (2) understand facts and ideas in the context of a conceptual framework, and (3) organize knowledge in ways that facilitate retrieval and application.
3. A metacognitive approach to instruction can help students learn to take control of their own learning by defining learning goals and monitoring their progress in achieving them.

These finding demonstrated that the processes of the mind related to learning are a far cry from the transmission model of teaching that has dominated instruction in the United States since the beginning of organized education in nineteenth century America. The idea that a teacher can tell students what they need to know, and call this "learning" on their part is in direct opposition to what the learning sciences reveal about cognition and its development.

On the bright side, however, there is evidence that many teachers, administrators, school districts, and policy makers are embracing the learning sciences and are designing learner-centered, rather than teacher-centered environments. Cuban (2007) studied pedagogical patterns of three metropolitan school districts from 1920 through 2005 and monitored their tendencies toward teacher- or learner-centered instruction. He used how teachers physically organized space in the classroom, how they grouped students for instructional tasks, and the activities in which students and teachers were engaged to determine whether their classrooms were teacher-centered, learner-centered, or what he called a progressive hybrid. In this study, he claimed that as a general rule, teachers were "hugging the middle."

> On the whole, the evidence I collected from reports on how teachers organized space, grouped for instruction, and the activities they designed for their students suggest that classroom informality and teacher-centered progressive hybrids I had noted throughout the 20th century in other districts have not lessened under district and state mandates but had even become more pervasive in these three districts by 2005. (p. 20)

Other evidence in scholarly publications exists as well. For example, *The Cambridge Handbooks of the Learning Sciences* (2006, 2014) provided a host of concrete examples of learner-centered practices that were unveiled in *How People Learn* (Bransford et al., 2000) and described the research surrounding their success. John Hattie in *Visible Learning* (2009) provided a meta-analysis of research related to many effective practices, heralding their success at improving student achievement. Schoenfeld (2011) in *How We Think* described how teachers navigate their way through decision making, and his analysis revealed many learner-centered tendencies. For example, his analysis of one teacher clearly described a learner-centered mindset:

> Nelson's orientation toward teaching, for example his desire to have students make sense of mathematics in contrast to having the mathematics presented for memorization, shaped his pedagogical practices. Specifically, Nelson felt that the ideas for classroom discussions could and should come from students-that in his lessons, at least some of his students would generate the right ideas and provide explanations of what they had done, which he then would clarify and expand on. (p. 76)

Schoenfeld's example revealed this teacher's promotion of students as owners of the learning and his desire to empower them, rather than to "teach" them.

Implicit theories of intelligence. Continued advances in technology and years of research by Dr. Carol Dweck of Stanford University and her colleagues added to our knowledge about how people learn and illuminated two distinct implicit theories of intelligence. The theories refer to two different assumptions people make about the malleability of the brain. Some see intelligence as a malleable quality and something that can be developed (incremental theory) and some see it as a fixed, nonmalleable trait (entity theory). These findings are summarized in *Mindset: The New Psychology of Success* (Dweck, 2006) and are termed "growth" and "fixed" mindsets. In short, students who hold an incremental view of intelligence or a growth mindset believe they can improve through effort and tend to pursue learning goals. They focus on learning new concepts and improving their competence. When tasks become challenging, students with a growth mindset appear to experience less anxiety, put forth more effort, and increase their engagement compared to students with a fixed mindset. Students who hold an entity view of intelligence or a fixed mindset tend to pursue performance goals; they are concerned with demonstrating their intelligence, getting good grades, and performing tasks that verify both intelligence and capability. When tasks become challenging, fixed mindset students often become debilitated and disengaged (Aronson, Fried, & Good, 2002; Dweck, 2006).

These mindsets influence student behaviors and their response to learner-centered instruction and must be considered as we navigate the complexity of effective assessment practices. In order to create an environment that is truly learner-centered, growth mindsets must be developed in teachers and students alike. Teachers with a growth mindset are more likely to establish classrooms that are emotionally safe, foster and support a growth mindset in their students by focusing on metacognitive skills and abilities that support learning, and by teaching in a manner that provides opportunities for students to show mastery of content incrementally throughout the unit of study. As a result, students can monitor their own progress and make adjustments as needed, consistent with the principles of formative assessment. Students with a growth mindset are more likely to set learning goals, monitor their own progress, and respond to feedback—all metacognitive skills that help students regulate their own learning. Students with a fixed mindset, even in a learner-centered environment, are unlikely to respond to efforts to help them improve throughout the year, believing that they are limited in their abilities and rendering the processes of formative assessment fruitless and vain.

A Portrait of Learner-Centered Classrooms

Then what does a learner-centered environment look like? If we build on Vygotsky's theory that students play an active role in the creation of meaning, along with the what we know about the malleability of the brain and its potential to be shaped by experiences, it changes the role of both teacher and student. The responsibility of the teacher shifts from one who "teaches" or transmits knowledge, to the role of designer, architect, and facilitator of learning experiences for their students—giving them opportunities to collaborate and co-construct knowledge.

Learner-centered environments include those in which teachers employ a socio-constructivist approach to instruction wherein they pay close attention to the preconceptions, knowledge, skills, beliefs, and attitudes that students possess and provide opportunities for them to construct knowledge through experiences—purposefully connecting new and old knowledge as they build on the interests, strengths, and needs of the learner. They are sensitive to cultural differences and theories of intelligence held by their students. They begin with where the students are on the learning bridge rather than where they should be and go from there. They use processes of formative assessment to make the learning visible and design instruction based on their evidence of learning. Students partner with the teacher and their classmates as active participants in the process and use metacognitive strategies to monitor and mediate their own learning as they close the gap toward achieving the learning targets. As can be seen, effective formative assessment practices and a learner-centered environment are inextricably entwined. A classroom that implements such strategies reflects a learner-centered environment. Just such an environment is required in order to have the opportunity to implement the processes of formative assessment, with both supported by a growth mindset in teachers and in students.

Where Are We Now?

Despite the abundance of information available to teachers about the learning sciences and how those practices should be realized in the classroom, instructionism persists. I would argue that it is the presence and pervasiveness of instructionism driven by cultural norms of the system and undergirded by behaviorist theories of practice that holds effective formative assessment practices at bay. Our classrooms are so deeply entrenched in the habits and traditions of instructionism that a folk pedagogy exists about what teachers and students are supposed to do in the classroom. Folk pedagogy, according to Ilić and Bojović (2016), is the lore of teaching based on lay theories or implicit assumptions that all teachers carry. Although teachers are exposed to best assessment practices through educator certification programs (ECPs), PD opportunities, books, blogs, online courses, and other media, and they do tend to have a basic understanding of effective assessment practices, classroom environments that support them continue to lag behind (Davis & Neitzel, 2011).

Conversely, critics would argue that many educators are, in fact, implementing formative assessment practices, but they have been distorted to conform to their pre-existing behaviorist theories about learners and learning. For example, Torrance (2012) and others (Airasian, 1988; Bennett, 2011; Klenowski, 2009; Marshall & Jane Drummond, 2006; Swaffield, 2011) claimed that in many cases, educators have taken the notion of transparency of learning targets and success criteria too far and made it mechanistic and prescriptive. In the service of "mastery learning," some have established a very strict set of criteria that serves as evidence of mastery, then coached their students extensively to get the results they want. This removes student autonomy and limits what success looks like and results in standardized learning outcomes and conformity. This behaviorist, mastery learning approach is what Torrance called "conformative" assessment or criteria compliance (Shuichi, 2016; Torrance, 2007), and it narrows the opportunities for personalized and social construction of knowledge. This incomplete, misdirected, or naïve understanding about the aim and power of formative assessment can result in the implementation of assessment practices that erroneously dominate instruction and rather than serve as AfL can result in what Almqvist et al. (2017, p. 6) called Assessment *as* Learning. That's not surprising given our history and tradition of working toward a one-size-fits-all, Tayloristic solution to achievement.

> Far from promoting an orientation towards student autonomy, such practices are interpreted as techniques to assure award achievement and probably help to produce students who are *more* dependent on their tutors and assessors rather than less dependent. (Torrance, 2007, p. 282)

Additionally, Torrance claimed that we have neglected the affective impact that assessment can have, especially when learning (or lack thereof) is socially constructed and visible within a "community of learners." Assessment is highly personal and can negatively impact a student's identity and feelings of self-worth, even in the best of circumstances. For example, feedback is often received grudgingly, even when coupled with positive comments, and many students may see themselves as failures. This is what Torrance terms *de-formative* assessment—something that must be acknowledged and attended to.

What Formative Assessment Is Not

Over the years, various components of formative assessment have been adopted by educators as a disparate set of strategies or tools to be used to solve achievement problems. This piecemeal approach to implementation has diluted (and perhaps negated) its effectiveness and diverted it from its original intent. To be clear, formative assessment is not a single instrument or strategy, but rather a process. The market is rife with formative assessment products that claim to raise achievement in the classroom and on standardized tests. One can purchase "formative and summative assessment bundles" that provide student worksheets and teacher answer keys in almost any grade and content area. "Formative assessment probes" that reveal misconceptions are also available as well as "formative assessment technologies" that provide instant data related to learning. However, each of these, although they have the potential to be part of the process, in and of themselves neglects the complexity of the process and is sure to lead to disappointment if used in isolation and in the wrong learning environment. For example, during a research study that I was conducting, I had the opportunity to observe in several science classrooms. At the time, the teachers were not privy to my focus of research and conducted class as usual. One of the teachers in my study attended a day of PD that centered on formative assessment. When she returned to the classroom, she announced to the students that because she was instructed to, she would be implementing formative assessment. Students were directed to fill out a self-assessment form as they took a multiple-choice test, then complete a test autopsy report after the multiple-choice test had been graded that listed questions they answered correctly and incorrectly, then determine if the questions they missed were simple mistakes or due to a lack of comprehension. Students were less than enthusiastic as was she. Once they completed the form, she reprimanded them for their mistakes, claiming that she had gone over that material and told them to "study harder" for the cumulative exam that was forthcoming. She then moved on to her next lesson, adhering to her carefully constructed lesson plan, neglecting to address obvious gaps in the learning. She later complained to me that the exercise was a waste of time and that students were not likely to take control of their own learning, and in this case, that was true as students rarely have higher expectations than the teacher for their own success. This illustrates that formative assessment is not a magical strategy that can be implemented on a moment's notice that produces immediate results. It takes time and a cultural shift to learner-centered instruction that includes the entire process as described earlier in the chapter.

Why Bother?

Despite the wayward application of the principles of formative assessment by some, the abundance of research that supports its use is robust and well-documented. Black and Wiliam opened the floodgate with the publication of *Assessment and Classroom Learning (1998a)* wherein some of their key findings examined various components of the process such as feedback (Butler, 1988), learning goals or targets (Schunk, 1996), self- and peer-assessment practices (Fontana & Fernandes, 1994; Frederiksen & White, 1997), mastery learning (Whiting, Van Burgh, & Render, 1995), and measurement and planning (Bergan, Sladeczek, Schwarz, & Smith, 1991) and provided convincing evidence that strengthening the practice of formative assessment produced significant, and often substantial, learning gains. Of particular interest is that so-called low achievers improved a great deal, thereby reducing the gap between low and high achievers. Some researchers (Bennett, 2011; Dunn & Mulvenon, 2009; Frederiksen & Collins, 1989; Messick, 1994) questioned the claims to effect size revealed in the studies, or their methods of obtaining student achievement data, nonetheless, the findings support a correlation between effective practices and achievement and thus warrant our attention.

Other studies conducted since the release of Black and Wiliam's research supported findings that formative assessment practices improved achievement and scores on standardized tests (Andersson & Palm, 2017; Black et al., 2002; Black & Wiliam, 1998a; Box, Dabbs, & Skoog, 2015; Box, 2008; Brown & Hirschfeld, 2007; Corbin & Strauss, 2008; Davis & McGowen, 2007; Fox-Turnbull, 2006; Furtak, 2005; Klute, Apthorp, Harlacher, & Reale, 2017; Li, 2016; Meisels et al., 2003; Passmore & Stewart, 2006; Rodriguez, 2004; Ruiz-Primo & Furtak, 2007; Weurlander, Söderberg, Scheja, Hult, & Wernerson, 2012; Wiliam, Lee, Harrison, & Black, 2004; Wilson & Sloane, 2000). John Hattie (2009) published a synthesis of over 800 meta-analyses related to achievement and academic success and cited a host of formative assessment practices that had strong effect sizes and thus a positive impact on learning. Self-report grades, providing formative evaluation, feedback, metacognitive strategies, mastery learning, goals, and peer tutoring all had an effect size on the achievement continuum of over $d = 0.05$ and were ranked in the top 36 out of 138 influences of achievement.

Conclusion

A convergence of negative factors—misunderstandings about how people learn, the need for standardization in teaching in order to handle the masses, beliefs about the role of teacher and student, and high-stakes testing have entrenched us in habits and traditions that are enduring and immutable, making it quite difficult to enact reform or change what is done in the classroom. However, knowing that formative assessment has great potential to raise achievement and instill, develop, and support self-regulation in students compels us to try. In the next chapter, we will take a deeper look at three classroom teachers and the context in which they worked, their levels of formative assessment, and elements that constrained or facilitated its use in order to make sense of the highly complex issues that influence teacher behavior and thus classroom practice.

Works Cited

Airasian, P. W. (1988). Measurement driven instruction: A closer look. *Educational Measurement: Issues and Practice, 7*(4), 6–11.

Almqvist, C. F., Vinge, J., Vakeva, L., & Zanden, O. (2017). Assessment *as* learning in music education: The risk of "criteria compliance" replacing "learning" in the Scandinavian countries. *Research Studies in Music Education, 39*(1), 3–18.

Andersson, C., & Palm, T. (2017). The impact of formative assessment on student achievement: A study of the effects of changes to classroom practice after a comprehensive professional development programme. *Learning & Instruction, 49,* 92–102.

Aronson, J., Fried, C., & Good, C. (2002). Reducing the effects of stereotype threat on African American college students by shaping theories of intelligence. *Journal of Experimental Social Psychology, 38*(2), 113.

Bennett, R. E. (2011). Formative assessment: A critical review. *Assessment in Education: Principles, Policy & Practice, 18*(1), 5–25.

Bergan, J. R., Sladeczek, I. E., Schwarz, R. D., & Smith, A. N. (1991). Effects of a measurement and planning system on kindergartners' cognitive development and educational programming. *Journal of Research and Development in Education, 29,* 181–191.

Black, P., Harrison, C., Lee, C., Marshall, B., & Wiliam, D. (2002). *Working inside the black box.* London: nferNelson Publishing Company.

Black, P., & Wiliam, D. (1998a). Assessment and classroom learning. *Assessment in Education: Principles, Policy & Practice, 5*(1), 7–75.

Black, P., & Wiliam, D. (1998b). *Inside the black box: Raising standards through classroom assessment.* London: nferNelson Publishing Company.

Box, C., Dabbs, J., & Skoog, G. (2015). A case study of teacher personal practice assessment theories and complexities of implementing formative assessment. *American Educational Research Journal – Teaching, Learning and Human Development, 52*(5), 956–983.

Box, M. C. (2008). *Formative assessment: Patterns, personal practice assessment theories, and impact on student achievement and motivation in science* (PhD dissertation), Texas Tech University, Lubbock, TX.

Bransford, J. D., Brown, A. L., & Cocking, R. R. (Eds.). (2000). *How people learn: Brain, mind, experience, and school.* Washington, DC: The National Academies Press.

Brown, G., & Hirschfeld, G. (2007). Students' conceptions of assessment and mathematic: Self-regulation raises achievement. *Australian Journal of Educational and Developmental Psychology, 7*, 63–74.

Butler, R. (1988). Enhancing and undermining intrinsic motivation: The effects of task-involving and ego-involving evaluation on interest and performance. *British Journal of Educational Psychology, 58*, 1–14.

Chappuis, J. (2005). Helping students understand assessment. *Educational Leadership, 63*(3), 39–43.

Chappuis, J. (2015). *Seven strategies of assessment for learning* (2nd ed.). Hoboken, NJ: Pearson Education.

Corbin, J., & Strauss, A. (2008). *Basics of qualitative research: Techniques to developing grounded theory* (3rd ed.). Los Angeles: Sage.

Cuban, L. (2007). Hugging the middle: Teaching in an era of testing and accountability, 1980–2005. *Education Policy Analysis Archives, 15*, 1.

Davis, D., & Neitzel, C. (2011). A self-regulated learning perspective on middle grades classroom assessment. *Journal of Educational Research, 104*(3), 202.

Davis, G. E., & McGowen, M. A. (2007). Formative feedback and the mindful teaching of mathematics. *Australian Senior Mathematics Journal, 21*(1), 19–29.

Draganski, B., Gaser, C., Busch, V., Schuierer, G., Bogdahn, U., & May, A. (2004). Neuroplasticity: Changes in grey matter induced by training. *Nature, 427*(6972), 311–312.

Dunn, K. E., & Mulvenon, S. W. (2009). A critical review of research on formative assessment: The limited scientific evidence of the impact of formative assessment in education. *Practical Assessment, Research & Evaluation, 14*(7), 1–11.

Dweck, C. S. (2006). *Mindset: The new psychology of success.* New York: Ballantine Books.

Fitzgerald, C. J., & Laurian-Fitzgerald, S. (2016). Helping students enhance their grit and growth mindsets. *Journal Plus Education, 14*, 52–67.

Fontana, D., & Fernandes, M. (1994). Improvements in mathematics performance as a consequence of self-assessment in Portuguese primary school pupils. *British Journal of Educational Psychology, 64*, 407–417.

Fox-Turnbull, W. (2006). The influences of teacher knowledge and authentic formative assessment on student learning in technology education. *International Journal of Technology & Design Education, 16*(1), 53–77.
Frederiksen, J. R., & Collins, A. (1989). A systems approach to educational testing. *Educational Researcher, 18*(9), 27.
Frederiksen, J. R., & White, B. Y. (1997). *Reflective assessment of students' research within an inquiry-based middle school science curriculum.* Paper presented at the Annual Meeting of the AERA, Chicago.
Furtak, E. M. (2005). Formative assessment in K-8 science education: A conceptual review. *Commissioned paper by the National Research Council for Science Learning K-8 Consensus Study.*
Gülpinar, M. A. (2005). The principles of brain-based learning and constructivist models in education. *Educational Sciences: Theory & Practice, 5*(2), 299–306.
Hattie, J. (2009). *Visible learning: A synthesis of over 800 meta-analyses relating to achievement.* New York: Routledge.
Ilić, M., & Bojović, Ž. (2016). Teachers' folk pedagogies. *Journal of Arts and Humanities, 5*(9), 41–52.
Klenowski, V. (2009). Assessment for learning revisited: An Asia-Pacific perspective. *Assessment in Education: Principles, Policy & Practice, 16*(3), 263–268.
Klute, M., Apthorp, H., Harlacher, J., & Reale, M. (2017). *Formative assessment and elementary school student academic achievement: A review of the evidence.* Retrieved from https://ies.ed.gov/ncee/edlabs/regions/central/pdf/REL_2017259.pdf
Lamar, S., & Lodge, J. (2014). Making sense of how I learn: Metacognitive capital and the first year university student. *International Journal of the First Year in Higher Education, 5*(1), 93–105.
Latham, G. P., & Brown, T. C. (2006). The effect of learning vs. outcome goals on self-efficacy, satisfaction and performance in an MBA program. *Applied Psychology, 55*(4), 606–623.
Li, H. (2016). How is formative assessment related to students' reading achievement? Findings from PISA 2009. *Assessment in Education: Principles, Policy & Practice, 23*(4), 473–494.
Locke, E. A., & Latham, G. P. (2006). New directions in goal-setting theory. *Current Directions in Psychological Science, 15*(5), 265–268.
Ludvik, M. J. B. (Ed.). (2016). *The neuroscience of learning and development: Enhancing creativity, compassion, critical thinking, and peace in higher education.* Sterling, VA: Stylus Publishing, LLC.
Maguire, E. A., Woollett, K., & Spiers, H. J. (2006). London taxi drivers and bus drivers: A structural MRI and neuropsychological analysis. *Hippocampus, 16*(12), 1091–1101.
Marshall, B., & Jane Drummond, M. (2006). How teachers engage with assessment for learning: Lessons from the classroom. *Research Papers in Education, 21*(2), 133–149.

McGuire, S. Y. (2015). *Teach students how to learn: Strategies you can incorporate into any course to improve student metacognition, study skills, and motivation.* Sterling, VA: Stylus Publishing, LLC.

McManus, S. (2008). *Attributes of effective formative assessment.* Retrieved from Washington, DC: http://www.ccsso.org/Documents/2008/Attributes_of_Effective_2008.pdf

Meisels, S., Atkins-Burnett, S., Xue, Y., Nicholson, J., Bickel, D. D., & Son, S.-H. (2003). Creating a system of accountability: The impact of instructional assessment on elementary children's achievement test scores. *Education Policy Analysis Archives, 11*(6), 9.

Messick, S. (1994). The interplay of evidence and consequences in the validation of performance assessments. *Educational Researcher, 23*(2), 13.

Mytkowicz, P., Goss, D., & Steinberg, B. (2014). Assessing metacognition as a learning outcome in a postsecondary strategic learning course. *Journal of Postsecondary Education and Disability, 27*(1), 51–62.

Nilson, L. (2013). *Creating self-regulated learners: Strategies to strengthen students' self-awareness and learning skills.* Sterling, VA: Stylus Publishing, LLC.

Passmore, C., & Stewart, J. (2006). Evolving ideas: Assessment in an evolution course. In M. McMahon, P. Simmons, R. Sommers, D. DeBaets, & F. Crawley (Eds.), *Assessment in science: Practical experiences and education research.* Arlington, VA: NSTA Press.

Popham, J. (2008). *Transformative assessment.* Alexandria, Virginia: Association for Supervision and Curriculum Development.

Rodriguez, M. C. (2004). The role of classroom assessment in student performance on TIMSS. *Applied Measurement in Education, 17*(1), 1–24.

Roschelle, J. (1992). Learning by collaborating: Convergent conceptual change. *The Journal of the Learning Sciences, 2*(3), 235–276.

Ruiz-Primo, M. A., & Furtak, E. M. (2007). Exploring teachers' informal formative assessment practices and students' understanding in the context of scientific inquiry. *Journal of Research in Science Teaching, 44*(1), 57–84.

Sawyer, R. K. (Ed.). (2006). *The Cambridge handbook of the learning sciences* (1st ed.). New York, NY: Cambridge University Press.

Sawyer, R. K. (Ed.). (2014). *The Cambridge handbook of the learning sciences* (2nd ed.). New York, NY: Cambridge University Press.

Schoenfeld, A. H. (2011). *How we think: A theory of goal-oriented decision making and its educational applications.* New York: Routledge.

Schraw, G., & Dennison, R. S. (1994). Assessing metacognitive awareness. *Contemporary Educational Psychology, 19*(4), 460.

Schunk, D. H. (1996). Goal and self-evaluative influences during children's cognitive skill learning. *American Educational Research Journal, 33*, 359–382.

Shuichi, N. (2016). The possibilities and limitations of assessment for learning: Exploring the theory of formative assessment and the notion of "closing the learning gap". *Educational Studies in Japan: International Yearbook, 10*, 79–91.

Sousa, D. A. (2006). *How the brain learns* (3rd ed.). Thousand Oaks, CA: Corwin Press.

Stiggins, R., & Chappuis, J. (2005). Using student-involved classroom assessment to close achievement gaps. *Theory into Practice, 44*(1), 11–18.

Swaffield, S. (2011). Getting to the heart of authentic assessment for learning. *Assessment in Education: Principles, Policy & Practice, 18*(4), 433–449.

Tanner, K. D. (2012). Promoting student metacognition. *CBE – Life Sciences Education, 11*(2), 113–120.

Torrance, H. (2007). Assessment *as* learning? How the use of explicit learning objectives, assessment criteria and feedback in post-secondary education training can come to dominate learning. *Assessment in Education, 14*(3), 281–294.

Torrance, H. (2012). Formative assessment at the crossroads: Conformative, deformative and transformative assessment. *Oxford Review of Education, 38*(3), 323–342.

Tovar-Moll, F., & Lent, R. (2016). The various forms of neuroplasticity: Biological bases of learning and teaching. *Prospects (00331538), 46*(2), 199–213.

Weurlander, M., Söderberg, M., Scheja, M., Hult, H., & Wernerson, A. (2012). Exploring formative assessment as a tool for learning: Students' experiences of different methods of formative assessment. *Assessment & Evaluation in Higher Education, 37*(6), 747–760.

Whiting, B., Van Burgh, J. W., & Render, G. F. (1995). *Mastery learning in the classroom*. Paper presented at the Annual Meeting of the AERA, San Francisco.

Wiliam, D. (2011). *Embedded formative assessment*. Bloomington, IN: Solution Tree Press.

Wiliam, D., Lee, C., Harrison, C., & Black, P. (2004). Teachers developing assessment for learning: Impact on student achievement. *Assessment in Education: Principles, Policy & Practice, 11*(1), 49–65.

Wilson, M., & Sloane, K. (2000). From principles to practice: An embedded assessment system. *Applied Measurement in Education, 13*(2), 181–208.

Young, A., & Fry, J. D. (2008). Metacognitive awareness and academic achievement in college students. *Journal of the Scholarship of Teaching and Learning, 8*(2), 1–10.

Zimmerman, B. J. (2002). Becoming a self-regulated learner: An overview. *Theory into Practice, 41*(2), 64–70.

CHAPTER 3

Embedding Formative Assessment: A Peek Inside the Black Box

Putting theory into practice is a complex and illusive task, and we would be remiss if we did not look deeply at the context in which teachers work in an attempt to make sense of it all. We will use the case studies of three high school biology teachers to illuminate the socio-cultural context in which learning takes place and will examine teacher tendencies toward learner- or teacher-centered activities and the assessment practices therein. These case studies and corresponding analyses described in both Chaps. 3 and 4 are excerpts from my earlier work entitled *Formative Assessment: Patterns, Personal Practice Assessment Theories, and Impact on Student Achievement and Motivation in Science* (Box, 2008) and *A Case Study of Teacher Personal Practice Assessment Theories and Complexities of Implementing Formative Assessment* (Box, Dabbs, & Skoog, 2015).

Case Studies Overview

All three teachers described in this narrative taught high school biology in a west Texas suburban community at Martin High School (MHS)—a pseudonym. MHS had approximately 1450 ninth to twelfth-grade students at the time of the study and a long history of academic excellence. Students at MHS were predominantly white (69.7%) and Hispanic (23.4%), with 22.9% economically disadvantaged and 8.2% classified as special education students. The teachers in the study—Phoebe, Mary, and Monica (pseudonyms as well)—used a common textbook and followed a curriculum map that school personnel had developed based on state standards. This map suggested a scope and sequence for their curriculum; however, teachers were given much autonomy in their selection of instructional strategies and frameworks for teaching.

MHS was under a system of accountability in which their exit tests carried high stakes at the federal, state, and local levels. Students were required to meet a minimum threshold score on the biology exit exam (among others) in order to graduate. Scores were used to assign statewide ratings and rank to each school district, and consequences for ongoing poor performance included potential state takeover. In addition, performance on these exams was used to determine a school's Adequate Yearly Progress (AYP) for the federally funded NCLB mandates that also included consequences for failure to perform and improve.

The observed teachers were not aware of the research questions or focus of the study. Ethnographic field methods such as observing, note-taking, video-taping, and interviewing were used to gather data. Each teacher was observed for approximately fourteen, 90-minute class periods that met every other day over the course of a semester. Although several lessons were observed during their comprehensive instructional unit related to the prokaryotic and eukaryotic cell, this narrative narrows the focus to a single topic that all three teachers taught over cellular processes including membrane permeability and molecular transport.

The following narrative will describe the educational background of the teachers, demographical information about their students, and layout of their classrooms, followed by a snapshot of instructional events that happened within their classrooms during the unit on cellular processes. (Readers of this chapter undoubtedly will have different experiences and levels of knowledge of cellular phenomena such as diffusion that are the foci of instruction in the three case studies. This should not be a problem inasmuch as the focus of the narrative is on what the teachers and students are doing as the topic is studied.) Throughout the observations, three instructional patterns emerged that were used to classify assessment practices: (1) teachers' tendencies to elicit evidence of learning, (2) their responsiveness to that evidence, and (3) their tendency to activate students as resources for one another and to empower students in their own learning (see Table 3.1). The evidence and significance of these practices will be discussed in the context of their teaching.

Phoebe. Phoebe, a white female, was in her 12th year of teaching at the time of the study. She held a Bachelor of Arts degree with a major in

Table 3.1 Rubric to determine attributes of formative assessment

Teacher actions that reflect attributes of formative assessment	← Higher levels of performance →		
	3	2	1
Reveals students' current level of understanding, needs, and abilities.	Consistently uses a variety of strategies to probe for evidence of student understanding. Probes may be formal and purposely embedded or informal and "in-the-moment." Probes are characterized by a high level of effectiveness.	Occasionally uses strategies to probe for evidence of student understanding. Effectiveness of these probes is mixed.	Rarely uses strategies to probe for useful evidence related to student understanding. Strategies when used tend to be convergent questions.
Responds to and builds on assessment-elicited evidence of students' level of understanding, needs, and abilities.	Uses assessment-elicited evidence about student understanding in an ongoing and regular manner that demonstrates responsiveness to student needs, builds on current understanding, and adapts instruction as needed.	Occasionally uses assessment-elicited evidence about student understanding in a manner that demonstrates responsiveness to student needs, builds on current understanding, and adapts instruction as needed.	Rarely recognizes or responds to student understanding in an adaptive manner. May recognize and not adapt, or may not recognize and therefore not adapt instruction.
Facilitates growth in the ability of students to take responsibility for their own learning and that of their peers.	Consistently uses strategies that encourages students to become active partners (with each other and the teacher) in the teaching-learning process by providing assessment and learning opportunities designed to foster self-awareness, self-reliance, and a community of learners.	Occasionally uses strategies that encourage students to become active partners (with each other and the teacher) in the teaching/learning process by providing assessment and learning opportunities.	Rarely uses strategies that encourage students to become active partners (with each other and the teacher) in the teaching/learning process by providing assessment and learning opportunities.

Table 3.2 Demographic information of Phoebe's students

	Female		Male		Both	
	N	Class %	N	Class %	N	Class %
White	7	38.89	8	44.44	15	83.33
Hispanic	0	0	2	11.11	2	11.11
African American	0	0	0	0	0	0
Asian/Pac. Islander	0	0	1	5.56	1	5.56
Other	0	0	0	0	0	0
Total	7	38.89	11	61.11	18	

English and a minor in biology and was certified in the state of Texas to teach both secondary English and biology. Upon completion of certification requirements, she taught middle school English for 1 year and science for 2 years at a magnet school before moving to MHS. She was in her eighth year at MHS and taught Pre-AP (Pre-Advanced Placement) biology and served as chair of the science department. She was also enrolled as a graduate student in a Multidisciplinary Science Master's Program that provided advanced content and pedagogical-content knowledge in biology, chemistry, earth science, physics, and math. Phoebe's second period Pre-AP biology class was observed and consisted of 17 ninth graders and 1 tenth grader, 3 of whom were classified as gifted and talented and 1 as economically disadvantaged. See Table 3.2 for demographic information regarding Phoebe's students involved in this study.

Phoebe's biology room contained individual student desks that were often positioned in pairs or quads that faced the dry-erase board at the front of the classroom. Her teacher desk sat off to one side. There were large laboratory tables at the back of the room where students conducted experiments and participated in group work, and equipment was housed in cabinets around the periphery of the classroom for ease of access. She used the dry-erase board at the front of the room to post homework and other assignments and to project notes or PowerPoint slides from her computer. Standards and overarching themes in science were displayed on posters hung around the room.

A snapshot of Phoebe's instruction on cellular processes. This snapshot chronicles teaching and learning events that took place across nine, 90-minute class periods and is taken directly from transcribed notes in *Formative Assessment: Patterns, Personal Practice Assessment Theories, and Impact on Student Achievement and Motivation in Science* (Box, 2008, pp. 82–87).

Day 1: To introduce the overarching theme of "form fits function," Phoebe provided pairs of students with a picture that represented a concept they had learned during the year. She asked them to think back and recall what they had learned about their assigned topic. After working in pairs for a time, she asked students to "stand-and-deliver" what they remembered about the concept. Throughout the discourse, Phoebe asked questions to help them conceptualize how form fits function in each example and then tied it to the form and function of a cell. This activity was followed by a brief PowerPoint by Phoebe that focused on the relationship between structure and function in a variety of cell types. She connected the new information to concepts learned earlier in the year about the characteristics of life including the role of the cell in living things.

Day 2: Phoebe introduced the "Plasma Membrane" lab to students that was designed to investigate the role of the plasma membrane in regulating the diffusion of molecules into and out of the cell. The experiment used a chicken egg (reproductive cell) as a model cell. She asked a series of convergent and divergent questions and built upon students' answers to set the stage for learning about diffusion. Students worked in pairs to set up the lab.

Day 3: Students worked in pairs to collect data from the "Plasma Membrane" lab.

Day 4: Students worked with their lab partners to analyze the data collected in the Plasma Membrane lab. Phoebe circulated among the students and guided them to link evidence to explanations through questions such as: What do you mean by that? What do we know about...? How do you know that?, thereby modeling critical thinking skills and processes. Important terms (diffusion, osmosis, homeostasis, and so on) were introduced within the context of the learning experience.

Day 5: Phoebe directed students to exchange and critique the lab report of a classmate other than their lab partner. Students shared the findings of their peers with the class, and data guided the direction of the discussion. Phoebe asked a series of convergent and divergent questions to help students connect evidence from their experiment to explanations about diffusion. Phoebe used the concepts students learned in the "Plasma Membrane" lab as a springboard for a brief lecture regarding the structure and function of the cell membrane. She provided formal definitions of key terms and other related concepts via PowerPoint presentation.

Following the lecture, Phoebe provided students the opportunity to apply their knowledge of diffusion and the plasma membrane within a new context through the "Diffusion and Cell Size" lab. The purpose of the lab was to develop an understanding of how the surface area to volume ratio of a cell changes as the cell grows and how this ratio influences diffusion. Students worked in pairs to conduct the hands-on part of the lab activity.

Day 6: Continuation of the PowerPoint presentation from Day 5 provided further explanation of new terms and concepts related to diffusion and osmosis. Then students worked with their lab partners to analyze data from the "Diffusion and Cell Size" lab. Phoebe circulated among students, both answering questions and providing feedback and guidance, and modeled critical thinking skills and processes through questions such as: What does your data say? What happened next? What does that tell us about rate? An optional homework assignment provided students the opportunity to relate cellular processes to medical conditions such as Cystic Fibrosis and others.

Day 7: Students worked independently to add teacher-prepared diffusion and osmosis graphics to their science journals. Via a whole-class discussion, Phoebe asked students to incorporate evidence from the "Plasma Membrane" lab and the "Cell Size and Diffusion" lab as well as previous lecture notes to construct an understanding of the role of the plasma membrane in diffusion. Concepts were extended to include specific conditions of diffusion including hypo-, hyper-, and isotonic solutions. Students struggled with the questions she posed regarding different types of solutions. In response, Phoebe drew several different conditions on the board and asked student volunteers to come to the board, draw their predictions about the movement of water, and justify their answers. Classmates were asked to agree/disagree with a show of hands for each student presentation. Students that disagreed defended their positions, and a classroom conversation continued until a consensus was reached by the students about the accurate characteristics of hypo-, hyper-, and isotonic solutions.

Students worked with partners to finish their analysis for the Cell Size and Diffusion Lab and answer questions. They were given two homework assignments; one required the use of the textbook to answer direct questions about cellular transport and growth, and the second assignment directed students to design and carry out an experiment at home that applied new knowledge about surface area to volume ratio in an authentic setting.

Day 8: Phoebe directed students to share how they designed and conducted their experiments with the whole class. The discussion focused on what they learned about surface area to volume ratio and how it affected diffusion rate. This student-teacher interaction provided "teaching moments" in which Phoebe capitalized, reinforcing understanding and helping students prepare for the upcoming test.

Students studied independently and then in pairs for the summative test. The 20-question, short-answer test included questions that ranged from factual recall to synthesis and application of knowledge. Upon completion, Phoebe led a whole-class discussion about which portions of the test they found difficult and why. Students joined Phoebe in coming up with ideas on how to make sense of difficult questions for the future.

Following that discussion, Phoebe asked students to complete a Learning Questionnaire and give her a "grade" on each assignment or activity related to instruction about the cell. Each activity or teaching strategy was listed, and students were asked:

- Did you enjoy it? Do you even remember it?
- Did it help you understand the concept more?
- What changes would you make to the assignment?
- Would you recommend that other students do the same assignment next year?
- Give Mrs. Phoebe an A, B, C, or F.

Day 9: Phoebe led a whole-class discussion about the Learning Questionnaire results, and students provided additional input about conditions that facilitate their learning. She then returned graded tests to students and led a discussion about concepts that students found difficult. She directed each student to complete a test analysis that included:

- A summary of questions answered right and wrong
- Possible cause for any incorrect answers (classified as "simple mistake" or "needs more study")
- A disclosure of how much time was spent studying for the test
- A plan for improvement
- Test corrections including an explanation of why the chosen answer was incorrect

Summary. Notice that Phoebe began with a planned formative assessment activity that was intended to connect students' prior knowledge to the concept at hand and was structured in such a way that it made their current level of understanding visible. Students shared their knowledge with her and with each other, and she asked probing questions to dig deeper so that she could respond accordingly. She activated students as resources for one another and included them as partners in the learning process in an emotionally safe atmosphere where critical thinking was encouraged and supported.

Phoebe sequenced the learning events in such a way that students were able to construct their own knowledge through experiences. They learned vocabulary terms and concepts during the course of instruction and thus in context of the content, rather than as a set of isolated facts memorized apart from the learning activities. She conducted brief and focused lectures *after* students had explored, building on their shared experiences to clarify concepts. Students were given the opportunity to apply their learning when she required them to design and conduct an experiment that drew upon their newly formed knowledge, thus allowing them to transfer knowledge to a new situation. Once again, learning was made visible as students described their findings in a whole-class setting. This constructivist approach to science teaching differs from traditional instruction wherein a teacher typically lectures and tells students what they need to know, then directs students to conduct a laboratory experiment that confirms what they have been taught.

The Learning Questionnaire that students completed on Day 8 is of particular interest. This metacognitive activity promoted student autonomy, fostering a sense of ownership and growth mindset thinking. A secondary purpose of the questionnaire was to gain feedback from the students about their learning styles and to assess the students' perceptions of the effectiveness of the lessons. This formative assessment activity provided benefits for Phoebe and for her students in several ways. Phoebe was able to use their feedback to adjust her instruction, and students were included as partners and active agents of their own learning.

Overall, Phoebe's instruction was very learner centered and constructivist in nature. If the aim of formative assessment is to empower students as self-regulated learners, and to create an environment that deepens the learning, then Phoebe's approach to instruction was spot on.

Significance of emergent assessment patterns. In Phoebe's practice, there was a healthy balance of the assessment patterns described in Table 3.1 including: (1) formative assessment practices used to elicit evidence of knowledge, understanding, and ideas (Category 1); (2) responsiveness to students' needs and the frequent linking of new learning to students' existing knowledge (Category 2); and (3) providing opportunities for students to take responsibility for their own learning and for that of their peers (Category 3).

Eliciting evidence: Category 1. It was common practice in Phoebe's classroom to participate in activities that made the learning visible, both formally and informally. She was purposeful in her design of such activities as evidenced in the stand-and-deliver activity that was used to draw out evidence of student learning and scaffold future knowledge. She used convergent and divergent questions to elicit information from them in order to gauge understanding. A classroom dialogue coding system (Box, 2008, pp. 94–95) used to analyze discourse showed that Phoebe's ratio of convergent to divergent questioning was much less than that of the average classroom (Wilen, 1991). Divergent questions have the potential to reveal a depth of understanding and a rationale behind student answers, thus allowing for a more nuanced adjustment in instruction by the teacher if needed, whereas convergent questions do not.

She asked students to design their own experiment, then share the scientific processes they used as well as their results, providing evidence of understanding, knowledge, and skills, rather than just declarative knowledge about the content. She served as a resource and guide for students during group work as they analyzed their data or solved problems, circulating among them and asking questions that probed for understanding or redirected their thinking when necessary. At other times, students were at the board, sharing their ideas, thoughts, and level of understanding, contributing to the teaching-learning process.

Although not described in the snapshot, Phoebe used frequent quizzes to identify where students were on the learning bridge. She used short-answer, free-response quizzes on a regular basis in order to determine students' level of understanding and to expose any misconceptions or errors in thinking that remained. She varied the level of difficulty, at times asking low-level factual recall questions and higher-level questions that required a synthesis of knowledge. For example, she asked the following: (1) Why are cells small? Be sure to use the following terms in your reasoning—diffusion, surface area, volume, nutrients, and waste. (2) Enzymes are catalysts. What does this mean? What does it have to do with the amount of energy required for a reaction? (Box, 2008, p. 102). Assessment-elicited evidence provided by student answers allowed her to respond to their level of understanding, needs, and abilities.

Additionally, Phoebe asked students to analyze their individual test results so that *they* could determine where they were on the learning bridge. The Learning Questionnaire was a metacognitive strategy that revealed evidence of learning styles and preferences as students were given the opportunity to reflect on their own learning tactics and contemplate classroom activities that they found effective.

Responsiveness to students: Category 2. Phoebe responded to the needs, understandings, and abilities of her students in a manner that is consistent with the tenets of formative assessment. She was purposeful about gathering evidence so that she could use it to guide her instruction. For example, the stand-and-deliver activity provided concrete information about students' prior knowledge about "form and function" that she could use to adjust her instruction as she wove their knowledge into a new context—the cell.

Phoebe responded to students as they worked together to analyze data by circulating and listening to their conversations and providing clarification or redirection when necessary. She asked guiding questions and informally gathered information that she subsequently used to inform whole-class instruction. She was adept at making learning visible, and thus was able to respond accordingly. For example, on Day 7 as students were synthesizing their knowledge about diffusion and asked to extend it to osmosis (the diffusion of water), students were confused and thus Phoebe stopped the planned activities to clarify. She drew the three conditions (hypo-, hyper-, and isotonic) on the dry-erase board and asked student volunteers to come to the board and draw their predictions about the movement of water in the varying conditions. They were prompted to explain their predictions to their classmates who used a show of hands to indicate their level of agreement. This activity was not part of her planned instruction for the day, but rather a response to evidence that she had gathered about their level of understanding.

When asked in an email correspondence about the Plasma Membrane lab, she stated that she had revised the sequence of her lesson as she sought to improve it. She stated:

> In the past, I have done (this lab) *after* they received notes…but I think this will work out well because now they all have a common experience to pull from when we start to talk about hypertonic, hypotonic solutions and details about the function of the membrane.

Her actions and comments demonstrated a shift toward a learner-centered approach to teaching and learning and that evidence from previous experiences caused her to adjust her instruction to enhance the construction of knowledge (Box, 2008, p. 104).

Also on Day 7, for those who had still not mastered important concepts, she gave them the opportunity to close the learning gaps through an optional homework assignment relating cellular processes to medical conditions. On Days 8 and 9, she demonstrated a responsiveness to the opinions and ideas expressed by students on the Learning Questionnaire and empowered them to be responsive as well. For example, several students found that using foldables to organize their notes was an effective strategy and as a result, Phoebe adjusted her assignments to include using foldables to facilitate note-taking on their next topic—cellular energy.

Responsibility of students: Category 3. Phoebe designed and implemented learning events that fostered a sense of community in her classroom and helped students become self-regulated learners by taking responsibility for their own learning and for that of their peers. Students spent almost a third of their time (29.33%) working collaboratively, either in conducting experiments, learning concepts together, teaching each other, quizzing each other in preparation for a test, or brainstorming and presenting their ideas. It is interesting to note that 12.39% of their time was spent in student-led discussions. She promoted self- and peer-reliance in a number of ways. For example, to promote self-reliance and a sense of autonomy, she consistently encouraged students to depend on their data as they made discoveries and drew conclusions about cellular processes. On Day 4 during the plasma membrane data analysis, she told the students, "Don't be afraid to think! And if you can back it up, write it down. Trust your data to help you make decisions" (Box, 2008, p. 105). Additionally, the Learning Questionnaire aided in the development of their personal metacognitive acuity, fostering a self-awareness about learning and learning styles. Phoebe also provided students a measure of control over their own learning by offering optional homework assignments that enhanced learning.

There were many examples of instructional practices that promoted peer-reliance. For example, students worked in pairs during the stand-and-deliver activity, designed and conducted lab experiments together, and critiqued one another's lab reports.

Mary

Mary, a white female, was in her 22nd year of teaching at the time of the study and planned to retire at the end of the academic year. She held a Bachelor of Arts degree in Spanish with a minor in biology and earned her certification to teach Spanish and biology through an alternative certification program (ACP). Upon certification, she was offered a science position and subsequently taught biology for 21 years and Spanish for 1 year.

Table 3.3 Demographic information of Mary's students

	Female		Male		Both	
	N	Class %	N	Class %	N	Class %
White	10	47.62	5	23.81	15	71.43
Hispanic	4	19.05	1	4.76	5	23.81
African American	1	4.76	0	0	1	4.76
Asian/Pac. Islander	0	0	0	0	0	0
Total	15	71.43	6	28.57	21	

She was in her fifth year at MHS and taught Biology I and Advanced Placement biology classes. Mary's seventh period Biology I class was observed and consisted of 16 ninth graders and 5 tenth graders, 2 of whom were classified as special education students and 8 as economically disadvantaged. See Table 3.3 for demographic information regarding Mary's students involved in this study.

Mary's classroom contained individual student desks that were placed in rows that faced the dry-erase board at the front of the room. The dry-erase board was used primarily by Mary to provide notes and diagrams during lecture, and at times to project PowerPoint slides. Her teacher desk was off to one side, and a stool was placed at the front of the room for Mary's lectures. There were large laboratory tables at the back of the room where students conducted experiments and participated in group work, and equipment was housed in cabinets around the periphery of the classroom for ease of access. The science lab and lecture area was large and conducive to investigations and group work by students. She used a large dry-erase board on a side wall to post homework and other assignments and hung posters around the room that described overarching themes in science.

A snapshot of Mary's instruction on cellular processes. This snapshot chronicles teaching and learning events that took place across ten, 90-minute class periods and is taken directly from transcribed notes in *Formative Assessment: Patterns, Personal Practice Assessment Theories, and Impact on Student Achievement and Motivation in Science* (Box, 2008, pp. 124–127).

Day 1: Mary opened the lesson on cellular processes with a lecture on the importance of form and function in cells followed by the history of the development of the microscope and the discovery of the cell. During the lecture, students frequently asked questions that drew on Mary's expert knowledge. As she talked, she used the dry-erase board to expertly draw illustrations and write down key concepts. Students were directed to copy the notes from the board into their science journals.

Day 2: Mary continued the lesson on cellular processes with a lecture discussing the structure and function of the plasma membrane and how molecules move across the membrane during diffusion. During the lecture, students once again asked questions that drew on Mary's expert knowledge. She spent time answering questions that diverged from the planned lessons but were related to the instructional objectives. While talking she used the dry-erase board to draw illustrations and write down key concepts. Students were directed to copy the notes from the board into their science journals and were assigned a "Plasma Membrane" worksheet for homework.

Day 3: Mary returned graded homework from a previous assignment. She provided students with the correct answers, which they recorded on their papers as needed. She continued the lesson on cellular processes with a lecture that applied what students knew about general diffusion to the diffusion of water in osmosis including hypo-, hyper-, and isotonic solutions. During the lecture, Mary introduced key vocabulary words and provided meaning to their individual prefixes, suffixes, and root words. As she talked she used the dry-erase board to draw illustrations and write down key concepts and students were directed to copy the notes in their science journals.

Following the lecture, she introduced the "Gummy Bear Diffusion" lab to students, which was designed to demonstrate permeability of a cell membrane and to distinguish between hypo-, hyper-, and isotonic solutions. Pre-lab instructions included a review of the formula and definition for the term "density." Student pairs set up the Gummy Bear Diffusion lab.

Day 4: Mary provided instructions for students on how to collect data from their diffusion lab and reviewed necessary calculations and clarified key terms. Student pairs gathered data from the Gummy Bear Diffusion lab and completed questions on the lab handout. Mary circulated among students and answered questions as needed. The questions tended to be procedural in nature. A post-lab discussion conducted by Mary ensued as she explained what results they should have gotten and what those results meant.

Day 5: Students independently took a "Plasma Membrane and Osmosis" quiz that consisted of 12 fill-in-the-blank responses (with a substitute teacher—Mary was on personal leave for the day).

Day 6: Mary returned the graded Gummy Bear Diffusion labs and discussed the results with the students. She paid particular attention to items that many students missed. She handed back the graded Plasma Membrane and Osmosis quizzes. Students worked independently to make corrections. They were allowed to use their books and notes and were awarded additional points on their test scores.

Following their corrections, Mary demonstrated osmosis in plant cells for students by using a flex-cam connected to a microscope and a monitor that enabled all students to see the reaction of plant cells when exposed to different concentrations of salt solutions. Students independently answered questions on a teacher-prepared handout. When all students were finished, Mary provided the correct answers and students graded their own papers.

Day 7: Mary continued the lesson on cellular processes with a lecture explaining how cell growth affects the volume to surface area ratio of a cell. As she lectured, she used the dry-erase board to draw illustrations and write down key concepts; students were directed to copy the notes from the board into their science journals. She then gave students a worksheet about diffusion and went through it with students, providing the correct answers as they filled in the blanks. Mary posed questions to students (that were on the worksheet) and had them raise their hands to answer. She used the opportunity to reinforce important concepts.

Mary then assigned a "Surface Area to Volume Ratios for Cubes" worksheet for homework and discussed with students what patterns would emerge as they calculated the surface area to volume ratio of different-sized cubes.

Day 8: (A substitute teacher gave students four worksheets to complete that focused on the plasma membrane and the transport of molecules as Mary was out on personal leave.)

Day 9: Students studied individually for their cell test, then took the 50-question, multiple-choice test covering the cell.

Day 10: Mary returned graded tests to students and led a discussion about concepts that students found difficult as evidenced by their responses. She directed students to:

- Highlight questions missed on their tests
- Write the correct answer on a separate sheet of paper
- Explain why they think they missed the question

Summary. This narrative illustrates Mary's approach to instruction and her limited use of learner-centered activities including formative assessment practices. Mary was extremely knowledgeable, had years of experience teaching biology courses, and relied primarily on lecture to transmit knowledge to students. She lectured very systematically as she moved students through the history of the scientific concept, explaining what is known and how it became known, then provided the content knowledge that she thought they should grasp, including key terms, processes, and significance. She structured the learning events in a traditional framework—lectures followed by worksheets or laboratory activities. She strove to apply scientific concepts to the personal lives of students in order to make them relevant, however. Her lectures were detailed and thorough, and she used the dry-erase board to diagram complex subject matter. She demonstrated a modest application of formative assessment practices as her lectures generated questions that allowed Mary to gather evidence of their level of learning and allowed her to be responsive as she wove their questions into her lectures and explained difficult concepts with a high level of expertise.

Students worked individually except during laboratory activities when they worked with a partner. Laboratory experiments generally had predetermined results and tended to confirm what students had been taught during lectures. Students were never directed to design and carry out their own experiments. A test review and a multiple-choice test typically followed the lecture/lab/worksheet sequence. Mary did not implement any form of pre-instructional formative assessment activities to determine what students knew about concepts before beginning or ask them to monitor their own progress.

Mary was a traditional science teacher who relied on an instructivist approach to teaching and learning. Students worked individually most of the time and sat passively in their desks, taking notes while she told them what they needed to know about the content. There was little evidence that students were empowered as self-regulated, life-long learners, or that they were encouraged to think beyond what they had been told.

Significance of emergent patterns. Overall, Mary's use of formative assessment as described in Table 3.1 was minimal. For the most part, her limited use of student questioning allowed her to ascertain their level of understanding (Category 1), and she was responsive by providing lectures that acknowledged and built on students' questions, interests, and levels of understanding (Category 2). However, she did very little to create a community of learners and facilitate their ability to take responsibility for their own learning and for that of their peers (Category 3).

Eliciting evidence: Category 1. The questions inspired by Mary's lectures revealed understanding by some students and occasional levels of interest in specific topics by select students—evidence that could be used to inform her lectures. At times their questions revealed high-level thinking on the part of the student. For instance, on Day 2 when Mary was discussing the structure and function of the plasma membrane and told students that molecules inside the lipid bilayer were hydrophobic, one student wanted to know how water molecules were able to travel through the membrane given its hydrophobic condition (Box, 2008, p. 136). This question revealed that the student understood the implications for water transfer given the hydrophobic conditions of the cell and the apparent problem it would cause if no provisions were made for certain molecules to pass through—an indication of understanding and interest. Even though approximately 90% of the talk documented in the classroom dialogue coding system (Box, 2008, p. 132) was conducted by Mary, she was always receptive to student comments and questions.

Responsiveness to students: Category 2. Although research has shown that the level of content knowledge held by a teacher is correlated to the effectiveness of feedback (Fox-Turnbull, 2006), content knowledge is clearly not enough. In Mary's case, her expertise was not leveraged to provide effective success/intervention feedback, but rather to answer their questions directly and thoroughly. When students posed questions that revealed their level of understanding, Mary responded by providing an explanation or elaborating on their existing knowledge, often relating the content to their personal lives in an attempt to make it relevant. Although it is common in a traditional classroom for a teacher to answer questions directly, this practice falls short of being considered "effective feedback." Providing an answer does not help the student know where they are in the learning process or give suggestions for improvement—it simply offers an explanation. Mary felt that being able to explain concepts to students in a clear manner was important. In a Formative Assessment survey completed at the beginning of the study, Mary was asked, "What are some factors that may cause you to deviate from your lesson plans?" She responded, "When students do poorly on something, I rethink of a way to explain it again," (Box, 2008, p. 137) thus demonstrating a belief that it was her job to pour knowledge into students and that she should respond when they lacked understanding. She also used the results of her multiple-choice tests to diagnose common problems that students were having and would re-teach those concepts. But as a general rule, Mary adhered to her carefully planned sequence of lectures and activities throughout the year, making few curricular or instructional changes.

Responsibility of students: Category 3. Mary frequently modeled critical thinking and scientific reasoning for students as she shared her thought processes during lecture—a practice that helps students develop cognitive and metacognitive abilities and thus self-reliance. Additionally, she assigned students to work together in groups during laboratory investigations (11.76% of instructional time), promoting a modest degree of peer-reliance. These student groups carried out the prescribed procedures, gathered data and analyzed results together as Mary circulated among them, and provided guidance when necessary. She encouraged them to rely on their data as they formulated answers and drew conclusions. However, students rarely collaborated on any other learning activities, being directed to work quietly and independently as they completed assignments.

Monica

Monica, a white female, was in her fifth year of teaching at the time of the study. She held a Bachelor of Science in biology with a minor in chemistry. Upon graduation, she taught for 1 year in Texas under emergency certification before moving to Florida, where she gained certification through an ACP and taught middle school science for 2 years. She subsequently moved back to Texas where she taught under emergency certification again, before completing certification requirements for the state of Texas the following summer. She had been a Texas-certified teacher for approximately 6 months at the time of the study and was in her second year at MHS where she taught Biology I and Anatomy and Physiology classes. Monica's fifth period Biology I class was observed and consisted of 19 ninth graders, 2 tenth graders, and 1 eleventh grader. Two of her students were classified as special education students, one as gifted and talented, and ten as economically disadvantaged. See Table 3.4 for demographic information that describes Monica's students involved in this study.

Monica's lecture/lab area was smaller and more crowded than many of the other science rooms in her building. Individual desks were positioned in rows facing the teacher desk and a large chalkboard at the front of the room. Laboratory stations lined the periphery of the room making lab work difficult at times due to cramped conditions. She posted homework and other assignments on the chalkboard and wrote her objectives on a dry-erase board near the door. A pull-down screen covered part of the chalkboard and was used, along with an overhead projector to display

Table 3.4 Demographic information for Monica's students

	Female		Male		Both	
	N	Class %	N	Class %	N	Class %
White	6	27.27	6	27.27	12	54.55
Hispanic	1	4.55	7	31.82	8	36.36
African American	1	4.55	0	0	1	4.55
Asian/Pac. Islander	0	0	0	0	0	0
Other	0	0	1	4.55	1	4.55
Total	8	36.36	14	63.64	22	

notes. A TV monitor connected to her computer was used to show video clips or other electronic media. She displayed vocabulary terms on a word wall nearby.

The following narrative provides a snapshot of Monica's instruction on cellular processes. Not included in the narrative is a description of the bell-ringer that she administered daily. The bell-ringer was a multiple-choice test question fashioned after their high-stakes exam, and the content was not necessarily related to the lesson of the day. After students spent time working on the question, she provided the correct answer and then went over test-taking strategies such as the use of context clues and process of elimination. This daily activity usually took approximately 15 minutes after which she proceeded to the scheduled learning activity for the day as described below.

A snapshot of Monica's instruction on cellular processes. This snapshot chronicles teaching and learning events that took place across seven, 90-minute class periods and is taken directly from transcribed notes in *Formative Assessment: Patterns, Personal Practice Assessment Theories, and Impact on Student Achievement and Motivation in Science* (Box, 2008, pp. 151–153).

Day 1: Monica opened the lesson on diffusion with a brief lecture and provided a handout entitled "Diffusion in Cells." She taught the concept of diffusion in a whole-class discussion as she guided students through answering many of the questions on the handout. Students finished the remainder of the handout for homework. During the discussion, Monica defined and described terms that students would need to know including diffusion, dynamic equilibrium, surface tension, and osmosis, and she elaborated on factors that affect diffusion such as pressure, temperature, and concentration.

She introduced the "Surface Tension" lab to students, which was designed to test the surface tension of water and the effect of additives such as detergent. Monica demonstrated how to carry out procedures and outlined what results students could expect. Students worked in pairs to complete the Surface Tension lab. She then facilitated a brief post-lab discussion and asked students what they learned about the properties of water and surface tension based on evidence gathered in the lab.

<u>Day 2</u>: Monica combined what students had learned about the properties of water during their surface tension lab, with their knowledge of diffusion to introduce a special type of diffusion—osmosis. As she lectured, she filled in the blanks on prepared notes using the overhead projector and students filled in the blanks on a teacher-prepared outline.

She introduced the "Plasma Membrane Model" lab, which was designed to demonstrate permeability by using a plastic baggie to model the plasma membrane. She asked students to make predictions about what materials they thought would diffuse through the bag (iodine, cornstarch, and/or water). Students worked in pairs to complete the lab. Students drew, labeled, and colored a picture of the plasma membrane in their notes while waiting for substances to diffuse. Following the lab, she facilitated a brief post-lab discussion and asked students to explain what they learned about diffusion based on evidence gathered in the lab. She assigned a "Diffusion in Cells" worksheet for homework.

<u>Day 3</u>: Monica returned students' graded Plasma Membrane labs and discussed questions that students found difficult as evidenced by their responses on individual lab reports. They turned in their Diffusion in Cells homework.

She conducted a vocabulary "Flag" game to help students prepare for a quiz. Individual students were given pink and yellow strips of paper that served as their flags. A definition was posted on the TV monitor, and two possible answers were displayed—one in pink font and one in yellow font. Students held up the colored flag that they thought corresponded to the correct answer. Monica briefly re-taught concepts as needed based on student responses.

<u>Day 4</u>: Monica returned students' Diffusion in Cells worksheet and provided feedback regarding questions that most students found difficult as evidenced by their answers. She conducted a whole-class review of vocabulary terms in preparation for the upcoming vocabulary quiz.

<u>Day 5</u>: Monica led students in an interactive vocabulary review game and briefly re-taught concepts as needed based on student responses.

Day 6: Students participated in another competitive game to help prepare for the upcoming test. In this game, student groups worked together to determine answers to questions posed by the teacher. Monica briefly re-taught concepts as needed based on student responses. The team with the most points at the end of the game received extra credit points on their test.

Day 7: Students studied independently for the upcoming test. Students took a test over the cell that included 9 fill-in-the-blank questions (a word bank was provided), 4 short-answer questions, and 23 multiple-choice questions. At the conclusion of the test, Monica briefly discussed with students the questions they found difficult.

Summary. Notice that Monica began the unit without implementing any form of pre-instructional formative assessment activity to ascertain students' prior knowledge or to connect with what they knew. She was a fairly new teacher and structured the learning events in a manner that was familiar to her. Her sequence of lessons alternated between lectures that introduced key vocabulary terms and explained scientific concepts and processes, with lab activities or worksheets related to the concepts introduced in the lecture, interspersed with games designed to make learning fun and to reinforce concepts. Laboratory experiments had pre-determined results and at times she told them what results they could expect to obtain, and at other times, she had them make predictions and test them. Students worked independently during class time unless they were in groups for a lab experiment or a learning game. Monica graded assignments in a timely manner so that she could provide students with feedback, and she responded to assessment-elicited evidence to re-teach concepts when necessary. She spent a good deal of time reviewing vocabulary and playing vocabulary review games to help students prepare for quizzes or tests as evidenced on Days 3, 4, 5, and 6. However, the weekly vocabulary terms were not always related to the content being covered at the time.

Monica's approach to instruction and assessment tended to be traditional and teacher centered, although there was evidence of a move toward a learner-centered classroom at times. Cuban (2007) would classify her as "hugging the middle" as she exhibited hybrids of teacher-centered progressivism as she attempted to empower students and create conditions conducive to critical thinking.

Significance of emergent patterns. Monica's use of formative assessment as described in Table 3.1 was situated somewhere between that of Phoebe and Mary. She occasionally utilized strategies that revealed useful evidence of student learning (Category 1) and then responded to that evidence to a modest degree (Category 2). Monica tried to activate students as resources for one another through occasional group work activities but fell short of creating a community of learners in which students were empowered in their own learning (Category 3).

Eliciting evidence: Category 1. Monica implemented a variety of instructional activities that had the potential to elicit evidence of knowledge. She placed a great deal of emphasis on teaching vocabulary terms that she thought students should know and the games she implemented often revealed what they knew and what needed work. For example, the Flag game on Day 3 helped her quickly identify vocabulary terms that individual students did or did not know. However, upon reflection, she recognized that this activity was not as effective as she would have liked. In an email that inquired about the purpose and perceived success of the activity, she stated:

> It was for review, review, review!!! I feel like I have to repeat things 100× in order to get these kids to remember anything! The pink and yellow activity was a review for their vocabulary quiz. Instead of just going down the list of words, I am constantly in the thinking process of fun ways to review. Since I had seen this at an inclusion workshop once…I thought I would give it a try. I like it, I just don't like that the kids are able to "use" each other's color so it is hard to get a true analysis of who knows and who doesn't. If this was an end of section review, I probably would have used something where I could really tell who knew it and who didn't.…So this game was so that I would know that kids were studying the right words and to give them some memorization strategies (you can probably tell that I am ALL about memorization strategies). (Box, 2008, p. 168)

This email serves as evidence that she had the desire to elicit evidence of knowledge, even though the activity was directed toward lower-level, declarative knowledge rather than understanding.

Students participated in other games during the unit that served many purposes, including eliciting evidence that Monica could use to determine what concepts needed correction or clarification. For example, on Day 6, the vocabulary game called for students to brainstorm answers with their team members to answer a question written on an index card, and points were awarded for correct answers. When teams were unable to answer, Monica recognized the need to re-teach the concept and gave a brief reminder or answered questions to clarify. Winning team members received extra credit on their test. Once again, this activity focused on factual recall, but it elicited evidence, nonetheless.

Additionally, she asked a few open-ended questions on the unit test which provided evidence of their thought processes related to the content, and she also, on occasion, asked divergent rather than convergent questions as evidenced by the classroom dialogue coding system (Box, 2008, p. 161). However, teacher-talk dominated instructional time, and students rarely talked about their ideas or knowledge for a sustained length of time. Although she may have encouraged or welcomed student ideas, they did not take advantage of the opportunities, thus limiting Monica's ability to ascertain their level of understanding.

Responsiveness to students: Category 2. Monica responded to student understanding to a moderate degree as demonstrated during lectures, lab activities, vocabulary games, and post-lab discussions. She used evidence of learning to sequence her lecture and lab activities and prompted students to draw upon their experiences to make connections about difficult concepts. For instance, she first introduced diffusion in a lecture that related it to their personal experiences, then guided students to understand the nature of a semi-permeable membrane through a lab activity, and finally highlighted the unique properties of water through an additional lab activity. Furthermore, she tied these three concepts together to introduce a special type of diffusion—osmosis, the diffusion of water through a semi-permeable membrane.

Other evidence of responsiveness existed as well. For example, during whole-class discussions following select laboratory experiments, she asked students questions about their data, prompting them to rely on it to draw conclusions. She then used their results to elaborate on the concepts, helping students build knowledge based on their own findings. Additionally, she routinely stopped the planned learning event to provide feedback and re-teach concepts when she recognized students' lack of understanding as evidenced in the vocabulary games. And in an email correspondence, Monica explained how evidence of student learning changed her instruction in a jigsaw activity (not found in this snapshot, see Box, 2008, p. 171) and claimed that evidence revealed prompted her to change her lecture in order to clarify and reinforce some concepts.

Finally, she revealed a tendency to reflect on the success of her activities and contemplate ways to improve them. For example, she realized that the flag activity was fraught with issues that limited its reliability. In the email correspondence provided above, note that she conveyed the desire to make changes in her instruction based on evidence gathered from students during the activity. In other words, she planned to respond to assessment-elicited evidence to change her teaching.

Responsibility of students: Category 3. Monica encouraged students to work together in groups during lab activities and vocabulary games (23% of instructional time), resulting in a moderate degree of peer-reliance and a sense of community. Although she did not promote self-reliance by allowing them to set learning criteria, reflect on their learning through writing, or ask them to write out learning goals, she did promote metacognition through conversations about difficulties they experienced on the exam as evidenced on Day 7.

Summary of Case Studies

Phoebe's use of formative assessment was the most frequent and effective of the teachers in this study. She consistently used a variety of formal and informal strategies to probe for evidence of student understanding. She was responsive to assessment-elicited evidence in an ongoing manner and shared the responsibility of learning with the students. The degree of openness, acceptance, and trust in Phoebe's classroom resulted in an emotionally safe, risk-tolerant environment where formative assessment thrived. Her classroom was learner centered as she taught from a constructivist approach. One area that Phoebe could have strengthened during the learning process was the promotion of self-reliance by students. Although she involved students more than other teachers in this study, she could have included them to a greater extent in learning and assessment tasks such as setting criteria, setting-specific learning goals, and formulating a plan to monitor their own progress.

Mary's use of formative assessment was limited. She rarely used strategies to probe for useful evidence related to student understanding. Direct teacher-talk dominated instruction without explicit attempts to reveal student understanding. Mary relied on her experience from years of instruction and assumed the knowledge level of her students. At times, however, she asked questions or students asked questions during lectures that revealed their knowledge. These questions provided Mary the opportunity to respond to student needs and build on their understanding, reflecting a modest degree of responsiveness. She rarely facilitated activities that enabled students to take control of their own learning; she valued compliance over empowerment. In fact, Mary felt strongly that peer instruction was detrimental to the learning process (she was afraid they would teach each other incorrectly) and therefore took on the role as the primary transmitter of knowledge. Her classroom was teacher centered and instructivist in nature.

Monica's use of formative assessment fell in between that of Phoebe and Mary. She occasionally implemented strategies that revealed helpful evidence related to student learning and then responded to that evidence to a modest degree. Most of her strategies revealed knowledge, rather than understanding, but still gave her opportunities to respond to student needs, abilities, and knowledge on occasion. She also facilitated occasional activities that encouraged students to become active partners with each other and with her. However, she neglected the purposeful implementation of metacognitive strategies that had the potential to empower students as life-long learners. She taught from an instructivist approach, and her classroom was primarily teacher centered, although there were occasional glimpses of learner-centered, constructivist activities.

Environmental Influences

Although all three teachers worked in the same environment, their instructional practices were very different. All three teachers (1) received much of the same PD provided by their district, (2) taught students of comparable socio-economic status (although Monica taught more economically disadvantaged), (3) had comparable teaching schedules, conference periods, and workloads, (4) worked under the same administration and physical environments, and (5) were given the same level of autonomy. Additionally, they all worked within the same cultural norms and expectations of students, curricular requirements, and pressure for their students to do well on the Biology exit exam. The environment in which they taught seemed to have little influence over each teachers' use of formative assessment practices. Rather, it was how they responded to environmental pressures (externally imposed contextual elements), guided by their instructivist or constructivist leanings derived from internally constructed contextual elements that seemingly had a profound influence on their practice.

Conclusion

Practices such as making the learning visible, empowering students as partners in the process, having students self-assess and set goals, providing effective feedback, and responsive instruction—all hallmarks of formative assessment—clearly fly in the face of traditional instruction and the long-established, deeply entrenched roles of classroom teachers and their students. As you can see from Mary's narrative, lecturing and direct instruction leave little time or opportunity for effective, ongoing assessment, especially for the student. In a traditional classroom such as hers, assessments are conducted by the teacher and are typically based on homework that students complete independently, or quizzes and summative exams taken in class that reflect individual mastery. Trying to embed the processes of formative assessment for and by students would then be awkward and seemingly intrusive. As you can see from Phoebe's narrative, learning environments that are student-led, constructivist, and collaborative result in conditions that are conducive to formative assessment practices, allowing them to be a seamless part of the teaching and learning activities.

As evidenced through an examination of the case studies provided, it is apparent that a variety of factors influence teachers' tendencies toward instructivism or constructivism and the implementation of formative assessment practices, despite equitable learning environments. In the next chapter, we will examine teachers' deeply held personal constructs that tend to influence their decision making and hence classroom practice.

WORKS CITED

Box, C., Dabbs, J., & Skoog, G. (2015). A case study of teacher personal practice assessment theories and complexities of implementing formative assessment. *American Educational Research Journal – Teaching, Learning and Human Development, 52*(5), 956–983.

Box, M. C. (2008). *Formative assessment: Patterns, personal practice assessment theories, and impact on student achievement and motivation in science* (PhD dissertation), Texas Tech University, Lubbock, TX.

Cuban, L. (2007). Hugging the middle: Teaching in an era of testing and accountability, 1980–2005. *Education Policy Analysis Archives, 15*, 1.

Fox-Turnbull, W. (2006). The influences of teacher knowledge and authentic formative assessment on student learning in technology education. *International Journal of Technology & Design Education, 16*(1), 53–77.

Wilen, W. W. (1991). *Questioning skills, for teachers. What research says to the teacher* (3rd ed.). West Haven, CT: NEA Professional Library.

CHAPTER 4

The Classroom Teacher

This chapter continues to follow Phoebe, Mary, and Monica, and reveals factors that influenced their decision making, putting those factors in a framework that allows an examination of the complex interaction of contextual elements both internally constructed and externally imposed. As will be evident and is assuredly already known, the teaching and learning enterprise is complex, and affecting change within an unwieldy system cannot be accomplished from the outside-in but rather has to start from within, and that begins at the heart of instruction—the classroom teacher.

THE CLASSROOM TEACHER

The critical role that teachers play in student achievement and academic success cannot be overstated. As designers, architects, and facilitators of learning, they are the cornerstone of formal education, determining what goes on in the classroom and ultimately deciding what students learn and how they learn it. Furthermore, teachers play a crucial role as facilitators of change (Battista, 1994; Cuban, 1990; McGrath et al., 2016; Orit Avidov & Tamar, 2017) and as a result are pivotal determinants of educational reform. As such, they are the ultimate interpreters of any classroom-based intervention and are directly responsible for variances in the effects of instructional interventions—known as the "teacher effect" (Fishman & Davis, 2006).

Study after study has shown that the teacher effect on learning is substantial and perhaps greater than the "school effect" (school choice) or other factors such as previous achievement level of students, class size, heterogeneity of students, or socio-economic status (Coleman, 1966; Darling-Hammond, 2000; Nye, Konstantopoulos, & Hedges, 2004; Wiliam & Leahy, 2006). Teacher effects (both positive and negative) are enduring and influence all learners, but have a significant impact on minority and low-income students who are the first to benefit from top performing teachers (Goldhaber, 2016; Nye et al., 2004). Conversely, Rivers and Sanders (2002) found that student achievement can be greatly harmed by a poor teacher and most definitely harmed by a sequence of poor teachers in a subject for several years in a row with potentially irreversible results. Therefore, the first priority for improving student achievement and reforming education is to change the nature of teaching and learning and what goes on in the classroom, starting with the classroom teacher.

That being said, changing the nature of teaching and learning is a daunting task. As noted earlier, many teachers find themselves entrenched in a system that is deeply rooted in tradition and cultural norms from which it is difficult to break free, if they desire to break free at all. Some teachers are quite content working within their comfort zone and tend to stay there if given the option. However, many teachers do change for a variety of reasons, such as a teacher's level of satisfaction with learning outcomes. Feldman's (2000) model of practical conceptual change revealed that teachers who are dissatisfied can and do change when given the opportunity. In an effort to improve instruction, they may informally participate in a type of trial and error, aptly named "practice-centered inquiry." In PCI, the teacher utilizes a specific approach, reflects on learning outcomes, and determines if the strategies were effective or not, and if not, adjusts their instructional practices once again in an ongoing effort to improve. This recursive PCI progression of implement–assess–adjust is a critical process that is necessary for reform as we will see later in the chapter.

Reform and Personal Practice Theories

As noted in Chap. 2, some states have implemented various types of reform, and achievement scores tend to correlate to reform efforts. While the findings are not causal, they do suggest that some schools are making progress. Unfortunately, however, as is often the case, reform efforts tend to focus on accountability and summative testing rather than the most critical factors to learning: classroom teachers and the context in which they work. Smith and Southerland (2007) asserted that:

Despite evidence that effective school change and new program implementation is more dependent on local elements within particular contexts (e.g., the classroom teacher, school administrative support, available resources, etc.) than on federal mandates or other top-down methods of promotion, reform efforts have traditionally neglected or undervalued the effects of such factors. (p. 397)

Reform efforts that *have* focused on classroom teachers, however, have revealed mixed results. Smith and Southerland (2007) reported that some teachers openly embraced reform-oriented practices while others did not, claiming that "reform efforts are largely dependent on teachers' ability or inability to modify their fundamental or central beliefs about what it means to teach and to learn" (p. 398). The implementation of formative assessment is no exception as it calls for significant changes in both teachers' beliefs, and how teachers view their role in relation to students and to the nature of student activity in the classroom. Therefore, if implementing formative assessment is a goal of educational reform (and it should be), then the beliefs and internal theoretical constructs that guide teachers' behavior including their assessment theories related to teaching and learning—termed "personal practice assessment theories"—must be addressed.

Personal practice theories. Personal practice assessment theories (PPATs) are a derivative of personal practice theories (PPTs) introduced by Sanders and McCutcheon in the late 1980s. PPTs are internal constructs formed over years of experience that underlie teaching behaviors and guide educational decision making. They include a teacher's pedagogical content knowledge as well as what they know about teaching, learning, students, curriculum, and the like (Clandinin & Connelly, 1996) and thus influence daily instructional decisions including how they plan activities and assess learning. Consequently, PPTs have a substantial impact on classroom practices and can be either positive or negative (Box, 2008; Gess-Newsome, Southerland, Johnston, & Woodbury, 2003; Sanders & McCutcheon, 1986).

PPTs vary from teacher to teacher and have their own unique properties. Consider the following examples. A research study by Cornett et al. (1990) described a middle school science teacher who was fairly new to the field. Her PPTs (in her own words) included the importance of (1) visual learning, (2) talking in kids' terms, (3) science learning as fun, (4) higher level learning, (5) very disciplined class, (6) reinforcing concepts, and (7) helping students save face (p. 521). She claimed that these PPTs influenced her decisions about curriculum and instruction and guided her classroom practice.

In another study by Sweeney et al. (2001), a novice high school chemistry teacher held very different PPTs, including (in her own words) the beliefs that (1) every student is a scientist, (2) science requires research, (3) students must learn and practice a form of the scientific method, (4) essential factors in a positive classroom learning environment include discipline and good order, (5) the classroom environment is critical to a positive, productive learning effort, (6) teacher equals motivator, (7) don't waste time, (8) students need a challenge, and (9) real-world applicability is part of understanding the importance of science (pp. 415–416).

Notice that both teachers addressed the learning environment and their beliefs about how students learn science, but their perspectives and underlying theories about the nature of learners and learning were distinctive. One would assume that these theories guided their practice, when in fact, instructional decisions are often influenced by theories that are not consciously held—a matter of propositional knowledge or the result of folk pedagogy. Or teachers lay claim to a theory, but their instructional behaviors are inconsistent with their claim.

Contextual elements. Beliefs that teachers hold, consciously or unconsciously, about learners and learning serve as internally constructed contextual elements that influence the development of PPTs. Teacher belief systems and how they influence practice have been the subject of numerous research studies over the years (Battista, 1994; Cornett et al., 1990; Czerniak, Lumpe, & Haney, 1999; Jordan & Stanovich, 2003; Proper, Wideen, & Ivany, 1988; Rimm-Kaufman, Storm, Sawyer, Pianta, & LaParo, 2006). Yet, while researchers have yet to reach a consensus about how to use the term *belief* in educational research, they have agreed that they are key determinants of practice.

In addition to beliefs, a teacher's knowledge is a key factor that shapes behavior and is central to the decision-making process. Knowledge is not limited to subject-matter knowledge; it also includes pedagogical knowledge. Together, these influence a teacher's PPTs. Furthermore, pedagogical content knowledge has long been suggested as a third major component of teaching expertise (Shulman, 1986). Pedagogical content knowledge refers to an integration of content with pedagogy, that is, a knowledge of the concepts, principles, and topics in a discipline, coupled with the knowledge of how to teach a particular topic. Shulman (1986) posited that there are three *forms* of teacher knowledge: propositional, case or theoretical, and strategic knowledge.

Propositional knowledge develops through personal experiences and through research into teaching and learning and represents the principles, maxims, and norms of teaching. According to Shulman, research-based principles such as active teaching, reading for comprehension, and effective schools are often stated as lists of propositions and serve as useful guidelines when making educational decisions (p. 10). Maxims, on the other hand, are practical claims that represent the accumulated wisdom of practice or lore of teaching. For example, "the experience-based recommendations of planning five-step lesson plans, never smiling until Christmas, and organizing three reading groups are posed as sets of propositions" (p. 10). Maxims appear to be the result of what Duschl (2007) termed folk pedagogy—a teacher's working notion of learning. Ilić and Bojović (2016) explained that folk pedagogies are implicit and intuitive, reflecting a teacher's cultural beliefs on teaching and learning (p. 44). Maxims may also be the result of popular belief systems about how students learn, that is, their mental model of learners and learning, and what teachers can do to improve mastery. And finally, norms of teaching include the "values, ideological or philosophical commitments of justice, fairness, equity, and the like, that we wish teachers and those learning to teach to incorporate and employ" (p. 11) and are at play when a teacher makes a decision because it is morally or ethically right.

Case or theoretical knowledge can be described as knowledge of specific, well-documented events that fit within a theoretical boundary that can be analyzed, interpreted, disputed, dissected, and reconstructed, reflecting the "how" of decision making. Thus, it is developed through a theoretical understanding of teaching and requires analogical reasoning and reflection. Both propositional and theoretical knowledge are decontextualized and often result in overly simplistic rules that are insufficient when placed in conflict with one another.

Schoenfeld (2011) in *How We Think* asserted that if we could understand the factors that shape behavior when unforeseen events arise, we could get at the heart of the moment-by-moment choices teachers make as they teach (p. 10). This is where strategic knowledge comes into play. Strategic knowledge emerges when teachers are faced with seemingly unsolvable problems where principles conflict with one another and there is no obvious solution. Teachers go beyond propositional or theoretical knowledge and use strategic knowledge to address these conflicts as they impose professional judgment and determine not only what and how, but *why*. It is what Shulman meant when he spoke of the "wisdom of practice" bridging the gap that exists between theory and practice.

Formation of PPTs. Teacher beliefs about the nature of learnings and learning, and forms of knowledge are foundational constructs of PPTs, yet it is difficult to pinpoint the origin and process of their formation. They take shape over time and according to Sanders and McCutcheon (1986) are influenced by experiences at home, experiences as a student, preservice preparation, and interaction with colleagues and other educators. "Some theories of action that are used in teaching are probably acquired early in life and come to be deeply embedded in the teacher's cognitive and behavioral repertoires simply through use" (p. 59). However, many PPTs are acquired on the job and are influenced by: (1) practice and the reflection of practice, (2) dialogue with, advice from, and observation of other teachers, (3) observation of and reflection on students and their learning, and (4) patterns of regularities within school life (Sanders & McCutcheon, 1986). Thus, the formation of PPTs continues as teachers reflect on the success of their experiences and those theories may be confirmed or modified, depending on their perception of the outcome. However, the process of teacher change is notoriously slow (Battista, 1994; Enyedy, Goldberg, & Welsh, 2005; Gregoire, 2003). Traditional instruction has been woven into the fabric of our educational systems since the Common School period in the 1800s and as such has strongly influenced beliefs about what it means to teach and learn. Belief systems that influence practice are often so personal and deeply held that they are difficult to modify, even when faced with research-based evidence that clearly contradicts those beliefs (Enyedy et al., 2005). In fact, Battista (1994) expressed alarm when noting that some teachers' errant beliefs caused them to implement inappropriate curriculum while simultaneously *blocking* their understanding and acceptance of the philosophy of reform.

As significant as they are, internal constructs are not alone in shaping instruction. Externally imposed factors "have a potentially powerful impact on teachers' personal theories about both content and pedagogy and ultimately shape teaching practices" (Smith & Southerland, 2007, p. 400). Externally imposed factors include local, state, and federal mandates such as graduation requirements, prescribed courses of study, standards, curriculum, standardized tests, grading systems, the inclusion of special needs students, physical environments of the classroom and school, and teacher preparation and evaluation systems. Frohbieter et al. (2011) found that curriculum pacing and class size, opportunities for PD, and access to assessment information influenced practice as well. Additionally, the social interaction that occurs with and within the physical environment between teachers, students, administrators, and parents must be considered. The socio-cultural context in which schooling takes place is highly complex—a "human-created environment filled with tools and machines, but also a deeply social environment with collaborators and partners" (Nathan & Sawyer, 2014, p. 25).

These internally constructed theories and externally imposed factors served as a mixed medley of contextual elements that influence "the methodology a teacher utilizes, his or her instructional goals, and his or her beliefs and knowledge about subject matter and its relationship to what is appropriate or inappropriate to do with students" (Smith & Southerland, 2007, p. 400).

Personal Practice Assessment Theories

Cornett's (1990) curriculum development model of PPTs was chosen as a framework for the multiple-case study described in this narrative. This model portrays the influence that external contextual elements have on teacher PPTs and the ancillary interrelationships between PPTs and curriculum, planning, instructional interaction, and reflection. Educational researchers such as Cornett (1990), Clandinin and Connelly (1996), Levin and Ye (2008), and Sanders and McCutcheon (1986) have used PPTs to explore and explain the complex interaction between teachers' beliefs, knowledge, and classroom practice. Cornett (1990) added clarity by designing a visual model depicting the impact of a teacher's PPTs when influenced by external factors on curricular and instructional decision making (see Fig. 4.1). According to Cornett (p. 189), in his model, the teacher's PPTs (E) influence their deliberations and decisions about what constitutes curriculum (A) for a particular subject and grade level. PPTs evolve as the teacher gains experience and as the context changes. As teachers plan (B), they are influenced by their PPTs which are continually impacted by external contextual elements (F). The external contextual elements that affect planning (B) also have a direct influence on the instructional interactional phase (C) during which students, teachers, and subject matter interact. Throughout the interactions, the teacher reflects (D) on the enacted curriculum which is once again impacted by the teacher's PPTs and external forces. The reflection may or may not modify the teacher's PPTs and curriculum decisions for the future.

For the purposes of this study, PPTs have been adapted to specifically focus on theories about assessment and have been termed Personal Practice Assessment Theories. I propose that teachers' PPATs influence what and how they assess and are influenced by contextual elements, both internally

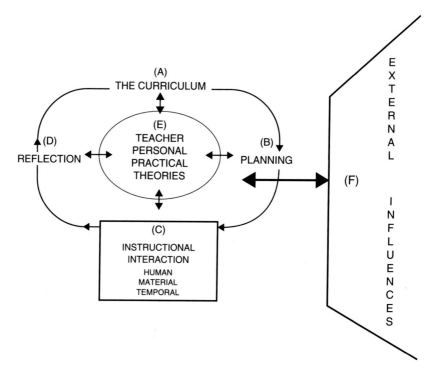

Fig. 4.1 Cornett's (1990) curriculum development model based on the impact of PPTs

constructed and externally imposed (see Fig. 4.2). In this Assessment Development Model (ADM), teachers' PPATs (E) underlie their decisions about the purpose (A) of the assessment activity which may be for certification or accountability (summative assessments), guidance of future instruction (formative assessment), fulfillment of a school mandate, collection of a grade for the gradebook, or fulfillment of an expectation related to normal classroom routines. Often, however, assessment activities simultaneously serve a number of purposes rather than just one. The purpose or focus of the assessment (A) is influenced by both PPATs and internally constructed and externally imposed contextual elements (F) such as high-stakes testing, administration, forms of knowledge, and cultural norms of the school among other factors. As teachers plan (B) their assessments, they are influenced by their PPATs and assessment purposes which have a direct

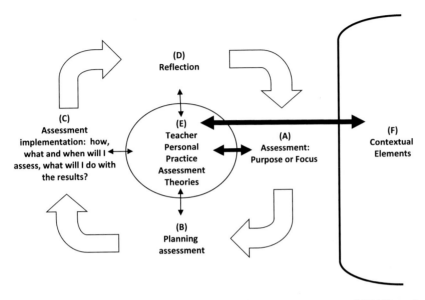

Fig. 4.2 Assessment Development Model based on the impact of PPATs and contextual elements. Modified from Cornett's (1990) curriculum development model

bearing on implementation (C), including what is assessed, the method and timing of assessment, and how the results will be used. Throughout the cycle teachers reflect (D) on the effectiveness of the assessment activity which may or may not result in a modification of their PPATs and assessment decisions in the future (Box, Dabbs, & Skoog, 2015, p. 6).

Data collection. Implementation of the ADM to address the research questions necessitated the collection of qualitative data related to the six stated components of the model. Classroom observations were particularly useful in gathering data related to B (planning) and C (implementation), while interviews and informal communications were useful in collecting data related to A (purpose), D (reflection), E (PPATs), and F (contextual elements).

Classroom observations. To situate learning events into context, each teacher was observed in their classrooms during instruction. Ethnographic field methods were utilized including the use of extensive field notes and video recordings, which were later transcribed to facilitate analysis. Profiles for each teacher emerged in a summary narrative that described in detail teacher-student and student-student interactions and the degree, type, and frequency of their formative assessment practices. The narratives were member checked for accuracy. (For detailed summary narratives, see Tables 4.2, 4.10, and 4.16 of Box, 2008.)

Teacher interviews and informal communication. In order to delve into teacher perspectives, a 90-minute, semi-structured interview of each teacher was conducted at the conclusion of the observation period. Interview questions were developed and piloted through an experienced colleague who was knowledgeable about the nature of learners and learning and was able to ascertain if the interview questions were "anchored in the respondents' cultural reality" (Glesne, 2006, p. 85), thus strengthening the potential for relevant, revealing answers. There were five primary aims of the interview: (1) to obtain background information, (2) to uncover both their beliefs and knowledge about teaching and learning, (3) to illuminate contextual elements that influence assessment decisions, (4) to identify and discuss PPATs, and (5) to determine the purpose and intent of specific assessment practices and the teacher's perception of success. All interviews were recorded and transcribed for use during data analysis.

The interview was organized into three parts in which teachers answered a series of pre-planned and follow-up questions (see Appendix J for Interview Questions Box, 2008, p. 270). In Part I of the interview, background information was obtained including their reason for becoming a teacher and how their experiences as an undergraduate or post-baccalaureate student influenced their teaching behaviors. Several questions were asked that were designed to illuminate beliefs about the process of learning, the nature of learners, their responsibility to students, and their perceived level of success. In order to identify contextual elements that constrained or facilitated the use of formative assessment, they were asked questions, such as "Are the assessment strategies and practices you tend to use now different from those you used earlier in your career? How?" and "If they are different, what motivated the change?" In-depth probing revealed their level of autonomy, the degree to which they were satisfied with their teaching, the system and their students, obstacles associated with high-stakes testing and accountability, organizational barriers, and attitudes and dispositions toward students and teaching in general.

In Part II of the interview, the concept of PPATs was explained to the participants, and they were asked to articulate their own personal theories about assessment. Their assessment theories were recorded and member checked for accuracy. Prior to the interview, our research team independently derived possible PPATs for each teacher based on analysis of field observations, data from the original survey, and informal interviews. Teachers were asked to critically examine the PPATs that our research team had derived to assess whether our observations and analysis conformed to their thinking and to confirm, qualify, or modify the PPATs as needed. After each teacher made the necessary changes, the two lists were combined, and the teacher then prioritized the list to articulate the PPATs each teacher felt accurately reflected her thinking and guided her teaching. However, as we analyzed their perceived PPATs, we noted that many theories they espoused were not evident in practice which led to additional analysis of the data collected in the study. As a result, only PPATs that were evident in practice were included in the ADM (E).

Part III of the interview was used to determine the purpose of specific assessment events, their level of satisfaction, and to identify contextual elements that they felt constrained or facilitated their use of formative assessment practices. In order to prompt their memory, teachers were shown video clips of their teaching and asked questions, such as "Do you recall what prompted you to use this strategy?," "What did you learn about students?," "What did you learn about the value of the activity itself?," and "Would you use it again? Why or why not?" This portion of the interviewed provided valuable data related to (A), (D), and (F).

Informal conversations before or after class helped illuminate the rationale for specific activities and allowed teachers to reflect on their success. Teacher comments were added to field notes and transcribed for further analysis. Additionally, occasional email communications provided rich, descriptive data that put activities in context. In both informal conversations and in emails, teachers would be asked questions, such as "What was your purpose for implementing (a particular strategy)?," "Was your goal accomplished? How do you know?," and "Did results of the activity lead to any instructional changes? If so, how?" Their answers provided insight into the reflective nature of the teacher and subsequent influence on practice (A) and (D).

Merging the data. Responses from interviews and informal communications, summary narratives of classroom observations, and physical artifacts were used to triangulate the data that was placed within portions (A), (B), (C), (D), and (F) of the ADM for each teacher (Fig. 4.2). (F) included both externally imposed and internally constructed contextual elements that constrained or facilitated the use of formative assessment such as forms of knowledge as described by Shulman (1986) that informed and guided their assessment decisions and behavior. Teachers' assessment theories in practice (PPATs) were placed at the center of the ADM (E) providing a theoretical framework for understanding the dynamic interactions between PPATs, internally constructed and externally imposed contextual elements, and the purpose, planning, and implementation and reflection of formative assessment practices.

Findings. Findings from this multiple-case study revealed distinct PPATs among the three teachers as well as several factors that constrained or facilitated the use of formative assessment in each teacher's instruction. Forms of teacher knowledge not only emerged as a critical factor in shaping assessment practices but also played a role in each teacher' ability to convert espoused theories about assessment into actual classroom practice.

Personal practice assessment theories and influential contextual elements. Phoebe's Assessment Development Model—Fig. 4.3. Phoebe's assessment decisions were informed and guided by two dominant PPATs: (1) Student understanding is enhanced if they participate as partners with each other and with the teacher in the learning and assessment process, and (2) Learning is optimized if the teacher assesses for understanding and adjusts instruction accordingly.

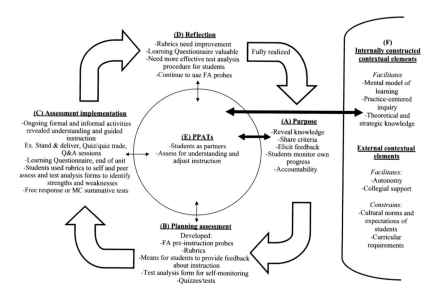

Fig. 4.3 Assessment Development Model—Phoebe

PPAT 1: "Community-centered environments involve norms that encourage collaboration and learning" (Bransford, Brown, & Cocking, 2000, p. 197) and was clearly exemplified by Phoebe's instructional practice. She connected well with students as she sought to partner with them in the learning process. Likewise, students partnered with each other at every opportunity in a wide range of instructional activities. They taught each other, learned from each other, served as lab partners to carry out experiments and analyze data, critiqued each other's work, brainstormed ideas, and prepared for exams together. Recall from Chap. 3 that on the first day of the cell unit, students worked as pairs in the "stand-and-deliver" activity. Not only did they rely on each other to access and probe prior knowledge, they shared their thoughts with the whole class as they engaged in discourse about "form and function." In this activity, each pair of students was given a graphic that depicted something they had studied earlier in the year where the structure of the object dictated its function. One pair of students had been given a picture of two types of plant roots, a topic that was studied during an ecology unit in the fall semester. Phoebe called on the pair of students to put their heads together to recall what they knew and then required them to report out. The following description (see Box et al., 2015, p. 11) provides a sample of the conversation that took place.

Student 1: We have taproots and fibrous roots. Taproots go, like, deeper in the ground for things that need water from like, further down and the fibrous roots spread out and they help anchor the plant.
Student 2: …and they also cover more surface area so that when it rains they get more water.
Phoebe: Oh, very nice…they have a lot more surface area. So, cool, if you can cover a lot of surface area and get more water, why don't all plants have fibrous roots?
Student 2: Because in some places it doesn't rain that much so they have to get their water from a deeper source inside the ground.
Phoebe: Ok, so you may find fibrous roots….do we find taproots and fibrous roots all the time in the same places?
Student 1: No…they're different.

Phoebe asked a series of divergent questions (why don't all plants have fibrous roots?) and convergent questions (do we find taproots and fibrous roots all the time in the same place?) during the exchange that were designed to make the learning visible and to draw out student knowledge.

Her questions expertly guided students toward the understanding that a common principle could be applied to roots and all other concepts students presented—a unifying theme in science of "form fits function." She built on prior knowledge and used evidence of learning revealed during their dialogue to guide the discussion as she helped them conceptualize how structure and function are interrelated and then applied the concept to the upcoming unit over the cell.

This approach to classroom instruction was typical of Phoebe's efforts to engage and empower students in the learning process and to elicit evidence of understanding. She sought their input about learning styles, habits, successes, and challenges and used the information to inform her instructional practices. Her classroom culture was risk-tolerant, open, accepting, and collegial as students worked with her and each other to reach their learning goals.

PPAT 2: Phoebe's lessons were constructed and implemented in a manner that led to a deep understanding of concepts, rather than a surface knowledge of scientific facts. Thus, both formal and informal assessments were designed to elicit evidence of understanding, and she used that evidence to modify her teaching in response. For example, consider the sequence and design of the learning activities related to the relationship between surface area and rate of diffusion. She probed for prior knowledge; guided students to explore scientific phenomena related to the plasma membrane, cell size, and diffusion; prompted students to explain their findings; and then required them to transfer their newly discovered knowledge to an authentic situation. They transferred their knowledge by designing and conducting an experiment at home that demonstrated the principles they had learned in class. This practice of "transfer" both facilitates and demonstrates understanding. Furthermore, students presented the experimental design, results, and conclusions based on their data to their peers and to Phoebe during a whole-class discussion. The dialogue gave Phoebe the opportunity to elicit evidence of understanding while also clarifying and refining knowledge. Lack of understanding revealed during the dialogue gave Phoebe the opportunity to adjust her instruction to close remaining gaps.

Figure 4.3 illustrates how Phoebes' two PPATs (E) were influenced by internally constructed and externally imposed contextual elements (F). Phoebe's mental model of learning resulted in classroom practices that empowered students in their own learning and activated them as instructional resources for one another. She understood Vygotsky's assertion that social interaction plays a role in development (whether consciously or unconsciously) and that students could learn from each other as they worked through their ZPD. She also recognized the value of making the learning visible and that both students and teachers could benefit when there was an open exchange of feedback used to move the learning forward. Additionally, her personal nature of discontent with her own teaching or student learning led to a recursive process of PCI. During her interview, when asked "Are the assessment strategies and practices you tend to use now different from those you used earlier in your career? How? If they are different, what motivated the change?," she stated that she assessed differently now than she did when she first started teaching. When asked what prompted the change, she responded:

> Exposure to what is good teaching. And just seeing that there were other things out there. But I've always changed. I mean, I am never, ever, ever, satisfied with what I do…you know I think that once you get comfortable, that's a dangerous place to be in education…you can't just use the same methods…they're different kids, we're at a different place, there are new developments…you can't just do the same thing. Exposure to what is good, and trial and error…that works. (Box et al., 2015, p. 12)

Theoretical and strategic knowledge also served to facilitate Phoebe's implementation of formative assessment practices. She possessed advanced forms of knowledge that served to carry her across boundaries of propositional knowledge based on folk pedagogy that often guides the decision making of many teachers. This knowledge led her to teach in a way that was countercultural to traditional instruction. Likewise, she understood *understanding* and made that her goal for students, rather than the acquisition of factual knowledge. Bransford et al. (2000) asserted that understanding requires the ability to transfer knowledge and skills to a unique context, which Phoebe included in her repertoire of teaching strategies. Her instructional decisions that provided opportunities for students to make this transfer were congruent with her PPATs and informed by a body of theoretical knowledge related to effective instruction.

Not surprisingly, the distinction between theoretical and strategic knowledge is not easily identifiable. However, strategic knowledge moves beyond theoretical knowledge when principles are in conflict and the solution is illusive. Many teachers, for example, rely on folk pedagogy when they succumb to "teaching to the test" as they believe that it is unavoidable in the current culture of high-stakes testing. Phoebe's students had to pass the state-mandated science, exit-level test in order to graduate, yet Phoebe drew upon her theoretical and strategic knowledge of how students learn to make instructional and assessment decisions rather than being driven by the test. Although standardized tests rely on individual accountability, Phoebe resisted the urge to have them learn independently, preferring instead to foster collaboration to promote learning. Her wisdom of practice overcame conflicting principles in a manner that promoted learning and was true to her personal theories of practice—evidence of strategic knowledge.

Several externally imposed contextual elements affected her use of formative assessment practices as well. The autonomy she felt due to the support from her administration and science department colleagues facilitated its use. Phoebe felt empowered as a professional to go beyond the norms of teaching in order to try new and innovative approaches to classroom instruction and assessment. She knew that she had administrative support as long as students were demonstrating success, and in addition, she felt a measure of collegiality with her fellow science teachers. She and teachers in her department worked well together unlike in her prior school where she felt reluctance to integrate novel approaches to instruction. According to Phoebe, teachers at MHS were "cooperative rather than competitive" (Box et al., 2015, p. 14), and this risk-tolerant environment supported her tendency to engage in non-traditional teaching and assessment practices as she worked toward perfecting her craft.

On the other hand, however, cultural norms and expectations of her students hindered her use of formative assessment practices. She discovered that students are equally entrenched in habits of traditional instruction and do not automatically accept changes in teacher practices or student roles and responsibilities, or if they do, it takes time (Hand, Treagust, & Vance, 1997). According to Phoebe, students in her classes had performance goals and worried more about their grades and how they compared to one another, rather than learning for its intrinsic value. Phoebe continually struggled to help students break free from their fixed mindsets and a "grade" mentality, to focus on growth and learning instead.

Curricular requirements and the demanding pace she felt compelled to maintain in order to cover them also served to constrain her use of formative assessment practices. When asked in her interview about the implementation of formative assessment strategies, she stated that at times this pressure caused her to be reactive rather than proactive in her planning and implementation of lessons and assessment. In other words, she defaulted to traditional habits associated with the need for "coverage" rather than teaching for depth (Box et al., 2015, p. 14).

These contextual elements (F) and her PPATs (E) had a direct influence on the focus or purpose (A) of assessment events. She used a variety of strategies that served to (1) make learning visible so that she could use the evidence to make instructional decisions, (2) share learning criteria with students before engaging in learning activities so that they could self- and peer-assess, (3) elicit feedback from students about the effectiveness of lessons, and (4) provide opportunities for students to monitor their own progress. As she planned (B) assessment events, she developed pre-instructional activities that were intended to probe for and reveal prior knowledge, rubrics that outlined success criteria, instruments for students to rate learning activities, quizzes and tests for formative or summative purposes, and a test analysis form for students to monitor their own progress.

Assessment implementation (C) correlated with the purpose of the planned assessment. For example, she used formal and informal activities that provided evidence of learning that she could use to inform her teaching. She led students through the process of using rubrics to self- and peer-assess. She allowed students to evaluate her teaching, facilitated opportunities for students to analyze their own progress, and administered open-ended quizzes for formative purposes and summative assessments for accountability purposes. She continually reflected on evidence of learning, and students reflected on their learning as well, strengthening their metacognitive skills while experiencing the power of PCI. Phoebe continually reflected on learning (D) and in her interview shared that (1) she needed to improve her rubrics so that they were more than a checklist, (2) she would continue to administer the learning questionnaire because it provided valuable information each year about her students, (3) the test analysis procedure needed work, because she was not sure how to help students master content from previous lessons once the group had moved on to new topics, and (4) she found particular activities very effective in making learning visible (Box, 2008, p. 221).

Mary's Assessment Development Model—Fig. 4.4. Mary's assessment decisions were informed and guided by one dominant PPAT: Students can demonstrate learning by recalling and applying terminology, principles, and concepts as explained to them by the teacher.

PPAT 1: Mary was a traditional teacher who spent approximately 60% of instructional time lecturing or leading whole-class discussions. The discussions typically included test reviews, "going over" correct answers on graded worksheets, tests, or quizzes, and pre- and post-lab discussions. In the pre-lab discussions, she often told students what results they could expect to get and in the post-lab discussions told them what their results

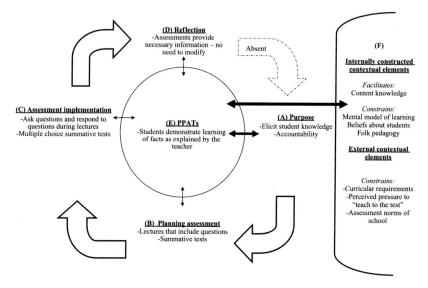

Fig. 4.4 Assessment Development Model—Mary

meant. For example, on days 3 and 4 of her summary narrative note that students completed a laboratory activity using Gummy Bears soaked in water to illustrate the process of diffusion. During the post-lab discussion, she explained to them what should have happened, soliciting very little from them regarding their own results. Then she provided an explanation of the process of diffusion as related to the gummy bears and to cellular processes related to homeostasis and kidney function. This prompted questions from the students as demonstrated in the following dialogue (see Box et al., 2015, p. 15):

Student: So, do you know about dialysis?
Mary: Yes, I do know about dialysis. Ok, dialysis is a process or procedure that is done for people when their kidneys quit working. Now, what do your kidneys do for you?
Student: They filter.
Mary: Yes, they filter waste products out of the bloodstream. Now let's understand what I mean by waste…

Mary's direct response took the form of a lengthy and informative explanation of the phenomenon rather than probing for prior knowledge and asking divergent questions that had the potential to reveal their level of understanding—a missed opportunity to assess the student's knowledge and make appropriate instructional adjustments. She continued to explain how the process of dialysis works, the role that homeostasis and diffusion play, and why filtering by the kidneys is critical to life. She drew detailed scientific diagrams on the dry-erase board and explained a complicated process, thus in accordance with her PPAT, provided students with the terminology, principles, and concepts needed regarding diffusion.

Student desks were arranged in rows, and they typically worked independently and quietly on assigned worksheets or took notes during her lectures. Occasionally students would pose a question about concepts presented in the lecture to which Mary would answer knowledgeably and thoroughly. Mary firmly believed that effective teaching was embodied in the art of explaining. This belief was confirmed in her interview. When asked to reflect on a lesson that did not go as planned, she described a genetics lecture from the previous semester in which she did not do a good job of explaining probability and chi-square analysis and stated that she wished she could have explained it again, but in a different way (Box, 2008, p. 140). Subsequently, in an effort to determine if students were learning, Mary asked them to recall or apply terminology, principles, and concepts that she had explained during her lectures. Worksheets typically called for low-level, declarative knowledge, and unit tests were multiple-choice that could be answered by factual recall or memorization. Additionally, Mary felt pressure to get through the curriculum and thus would often ask and answer her own questions during lectures if students were hesitant or slow to respond, reverting to her default mode of "explaining" what she thought they needed to know.

Figure 4.4 illustrates how Mary's PPAT (E) was influenced predominantly by constraining contextual elements (F). Her extensive content knowledge could have been leveraged to generate deep, rich discussions that involved students and probed their levels of understanding. However, her mental model of how students learn hindered her from involving them as partners and co-constructers of knowledge, thus limiting her use of learner-centered, formative assessment practices. When asked about learning in an interview, Mary claimed that relevance was the key to opening minds, and then it was her job to fill those minds with knowledge. She felt that it was her duty and obligation to explain difficult concepts, rather than provide experiences that allowed them to construct knowledge on their own or with the help of peers. Furthermore, she thought that many students were apathetic and not inclined to put forth the effort necessary for them to construct knowledge. When asked about the possibility of using inquiry-based learning, she stated:

> I would love to be able to start off the school year with just a simple little problem and get the kids in groups and say, I need you to figure out how to solve this. And let the kids start brainstorming. But once again, the kids are like, oh god if it takes much effort, they are like "I don't want to do this, this is too hard," they'll say. (Box et al., 2015, p. 17)

She also stated in her interview that she approached instruction differently for advanced-placement biology students than she did for her current "regular" on-level students who she described as unmotivated and not likely to be self-directed enough to complete assignments (Box, 2008, p. 217). Her low expectations for on-level biology students influenced her decision making, further reinforcing the perceived need for traditional instruction, thus she continued to adhere to the tenets of instructivism.

Mary's PPAT was informed by propositional knowledge in the form of folk pedagogy as reflected in specific maxims revealed in her practice. When asked about assessment practices, she claimed that the end-of-year, high-stakes test drove her assessment decisions. Even though she claimed she knew how to teach for understanding and assess accordingly, she was driven by the test, which in her mind relied on factual, surface knowledge. When asked what impact her views on how students learn influenced her assessment strategies, she stated:

> It probably doesn't influence my assessment strategies that much, because even though there's lots of this stuff that I teach that's relevant, but there's all that other stuff that unfortunately, I'm driven by the TAKS test...going, they (students) may not think it's relevant, but by god it is for the test so I need to put it on my assessment. (Box et al., 2015, p. 17)

A convergence of factors resulted in Mary's instructivistic approach to teaching and learning and thus served as justification for putting this theory into practice. Her propositional knowledge about how students learn, what she thought students needed to know to pass the end-of-year exam, and her perceived role as an educator undergirded decision making and informed her practice. Mary was highly intelligent and had accumulated a wealth of content knowledge throughout her teaching career. Her experiences convinced her that the best way to share that knowledge was through the process of clear and concise explanation. This instructivist approach to education places a high value on content and makes the learner the target of instruction (Cannings & Stager, 2003, p. 2) rather than facilitating the personal construction of knowledge through experiences. Her lectures were designed to transmit facts, principles, concepts, and the application of concepts that she wanted students to know for the test. In her mind, the perceived goals of education in light of high-stakes exams existed without conflict with her propositional knowledge about how students learn science. Her belief that tests required factual recall reinforced her teaching and assessment approach.

Like Phoebe, Mary felt pressure to cover the entire required curriculum. She also had a clear desire to help students be successful on the end-of-year, high-stakes exam, claiming that she felt obligated to "teach to the test" even though she thought students would learn best through inquiry. Although she was familiar with the concept of inquiry-based learning, she stated that most of her students could not conduct inquiry experiments because they had been "spoon-fed rote memorization and don't know how to think" and that students should develop problem-solving skills, but at her school that was "just not how science is mainly taught" (Box et al., 2015, p. 18).

These contextual elements (F) and her PPATs (E) influenced her decisions about the purpose or focus (A) of assessment events. Mary focused on summative assessments with the exception of informal assessments made of student knowledge through question and answer sessions during lectures. She planned (B) and implemented (C) summative multiple-choice exams that used the same format as the end-of-year, high-stakes exam in order to prepare them. When she evaluated homework, labs, or tests, she used evidence of learning to recognize where students struggled and then provided feedback in a whole-class setting, explaining concepts again when needed. As she reflected (D) on the effectiveness of her instruction, she was satisfied that her assessments provided needed information and there was no evidence during this study that Mary's reflection on student learning changed her mode of instruction or assessment practices.

Monica's Assessment Development Model—Fig. 4.5. Monica's assessment decisions were informed and guided by two dominant PPATs: (1) Students can demonstrate learning in a variety of ways, and (2) Students' knowledge of scientific facts provides evidence of learning about science and the natural world.

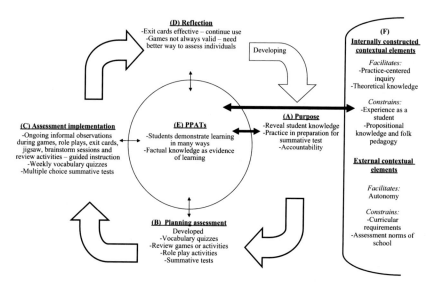

Fig. 4.5 Assessment Development Model—Monica

PPAT 1: During the cell unit, Monica frequently varied her activities which allowed students to demonstrate learning in an assortment of contexts through various modes, other than paper and pencil tests. She elicited evidence of knowledge through activities such as role-plays, laboratory activities, quizzes and tests, worksheets, exit cards, vocabulary games, a jigsaw activity, and a concept attainment activity (see summary narrative, Box, 2008, pp. 152–156); however, most of the evidence elicited tended to be at the factual rather than conceptual level. Propositional knowledge from a normative perspective of justice, fairness, and equity informed and shaped her practice. She stated in her interview that she thought all students could "prove learning to you in one way or another," so to be fair, she offered a variety of ways for them to demonstrate their knowledge.

PPAT 2: Monica operated from the premise that students should memorize scientific vocabulary terms and processes and be able to recall what they had committed to memory. Her job was to deliver the content in a way that would facilitate their ability to recall. Each day during instruction, students participated in a bell-ringer that focused on vocabulary and its use in context of a question. She followed her lectures with review games that reinforced the memorization of terms. Although she focused a great deal on vocabulary, in her interview she expressed the belief that she should do more but felt constrained by time. However, at a minimum, she felt that vocabulary was important so that students were able to "speak the language...they have to know the stuff to be able to talk about it" (Box, 2008, pp. 174–175).

She was familiar with inquiry-based learning and stated that she would love to teach through inquiry so that students could learn with understanding, but inquiry lessons would put her "five class periods behind....I don't have five class periods, then I'm three chapters behind...with the amount of content (required to cover as dictated by the consensus map), you can't do that" (Box et al., 2015, p. 19). Thus, her assessments focused on students' ability to use terms and concepts she had presented during lecture rather than on their ability to use them in new contexts or to solve problems—a more efficient use of time.

Figure 4.5 illustrates how Monica's two PPATs (E) were influenced by both facilitating and constraining contextual elements (F). Monica's tendency to engage in PCI was a positive influence and resulted in a modest use of formative assessment or other learner-centered practices. As a beginning teacher, she was receptive to new ideas and was working to add to her repertoire of strategies. She was reflective and adaptive. When evidence suggested that students were not learning as much as she thought they should, she tried new and different approaches to instruction—usually ones that she had learned at workshops or from other colleagues.

There was evidence that Monica implemented strategies that were informed by and aligned with theoretical knowledge that undergirds formative assessment practices. Monica stated in her interview, "Assessment is about acknowledging whether or not a student has learned with understanding." She further asserted, "I would love to teach *thinking* rather than vocabulary" (Box, 2008, p. 177). She understood what and how she should teach and assess students but was unable to free herself from the cultural norms that have had a strong influence on science education for many years.

Many of her instructional decisions appeared to be guided by folk pedagogy and maxims that represented the conventional wisdom she had gained through her experiences as a student. In her interview, Monica stated that she was a "great memorizer" in high school and college (Box et al., 2015, p. 20) and those abilities sustained her. She was able to be a high achiever without actually developing a deep understanding of the content, as is frequently the case in traditional science instruction. Thus, her personal experiences as a student stood juxtaposed with the concept of teaching for understanding and served as a barrier to transforming her espoused beliefs about teaching for understanding into actual practice. Under pressure to succeed, she defaulted to teaching in a manner that was familiar to her, which was usually teacher- rather than learner-centered.

Although Monica tended to teach from an instructivist approach, there were times when she demonstrated a shift toward learner-centered instruction that led to a deeper understanding of cellular biology concepts. For example, she used a jigsaw activity to teach students about the importance of photosynthesis. Students were assigned a "home" group, then split off into "expert" groups, each of which was assigned a different part of an article entitled *Why Study Photosynthesis?* In their expert groups, they were instructed to discuss the reading and then work as a team to answer questions about the assignment on a teacher-prepared handout. After becoming familiar with the material, they returned to their home group and shared what they had learned with their peers. Since each member of the home group had studied a different segment, they were able to discuss the entire article and fill in answers to all of the questions on the handout—learning from each other. Monica followed the activity with a discussion, leading up to a lecture that built on what they had discussed in their groups (see Box et al., 2015, p. 21).

Monica:	Tell me why we should study photosynthesis? Why should we care?
Student 1:	Well, because photosynthesis is used to make a lot of our things like clothes, or used to power our cars by like it said, by fossil fuels that are there because plants were, like basically under the ground for millions of years.
Monica:	Yes, right. Guys, this group had an interesting reading and it took us back to our earth science days. It talked about coal—fossil fuels are actually made from dead things, plants and animals that have been under the ground for millions of years…without plants, it would be difficult to power so many things that we have because of the electricity, running our cars—we wouldn't have any fuel for it. What else?
Student 2:	They give us oxygen, produce oxygen for us to breathe.
Monica:	You're right, without photosynthesis, not only would we die because we didn't have anything to eat, but we would also suffocate with no oxygen.

In this activity, Monica activated students as resources for each other and fostered collaboration—a learner-centered approach to instruction. Notice that she used divergent questions to elicit evidence from students that set the stage for knowledge construction. From there, Monica explained to students that they needed to study adenosine-tri-phosphate, an important energy molecule. This activity and exit cards used at the end of class resulted in a degree of conceptual understanding by students and made learning visible, allowing Monica an opportunity to assess student learning and adjust as needed.

But as a general rule, more contextual elements constrained than facilitated her use of formative assessment practices. She expressed that she had a great deal of freedom and autonomy—a condition that should have encouraged her to try more learner-centered strategies, yet most of the time she did what she thought was expected. Data from the initial survey provided evidence that her assessment practices were consistent with most teachers at her school where many other science teachers were hugging the middle. Additionally, she defaulted to traditional instruction that she had experienced as a student. Although at times theoretical knowledge influenced her decision making, that knowledge clashed with the maxims that she held about the importance of memorization, the need to cover the curriculum, and the responsibility to prepare students for the high-stakes exam. The cognitive dissonance created by the gap between her theory and practice caused her to try new assessment and teaching strategies in an attempt to narrow or close this gap.

These contextual elements (F) and her PPATs (E) influenced her decisions about the focus and purpose (A) of assessment events. Most of Monica's informal assessment events were designed to elicit evidence of knowledge so that she could provide verbal feedback and help them prepare for summative tests, which were then used for accountability purposes. Therefore, Monica planned (B) vocabulary quizzes, review games, or other creative activities that would allow students to demonstrate learning in different ways, and multiple-choice summative exams. When assessments were implemented (C), she assessed both through formal and informal means. She continually evaluated student's declarative knowledge and was responsive to informal assessment events by providing verbal feedback to individual students or would re-teach concepts in a whole-class setting when necessary. Monica was reflective and was developing a sense of the power of PCI. As she reflected on her assessment practices, (D) she felt that the exit cards were an effective means of revealing comprehension, and that conversely, some of her chosen games and activities were not very effective in demonstrating individual knowledge. She recognized that some strategies were ineffective and incongruent with her theoretical knowledge about teaching for understanding and was committed to learning new approaches to alleviate or eliminate this discrepancy.

SUMMARY

Table 4.1 provides a summary of the three teachers' PPATs, their forms of knowledge, and contextual elements that appeared to facilitate or constrain their use of formative assessment.

Table 4.1 Assessment Development Model summary

	Phoebe	Mary	Monica
Personal practice assessment theories	1. Student understanding is enhanced if students participate as partners with each other and with the teacher in the learning and assessment process 2. Learning is optimized if the teacher assesses for understanding and adjusts instruction accordingly	1. Students demonstrate learning by recalling and applying terminology, principles, and concepts as explained to them by the teacher	1. Students can demonstrate learning in a variety of ways 2. Students' knowledge of scientific facts provides evidence of learning about science and the natural world
Dominant forms of knowledge	Theoretical and strategic	Practical knowledge and maxims (propositional)	Practical (propositional) and theoretical
Contextual elements that constrain	1. Cultural norms experienced by students 2. Pace of instruction due to state and local curriculum requirements	1. Mental model of learning 2. Beliefs about student motivation and effort 3. Teaching to the test and need for "coverage"	1. Experiences as a student 2. Assessment norms of the school 3. Teaching to the test and need for "coverage"
Contextual elements that facilitate	1. Mental model of learning 2. Perceived autonomy 3. Support from colleagues 4. Practice-centered inquiry	1. Knowledge of the subject matter	1. Practice-centered inquiry 2. Perceived autonomy

Personal practice assessment theories. Analysis of the data revealed that Mary and Monica held PPATs that were similar to each other in some respects. They were both guided by the theory that students learn science through the accumulation of facts and knowledge. Despite the initial similarities, other PPATs emerged during this study were distinctly different from one another. Monica held a PPAT that students could demonstrate their knowledge through a variety of ways, and Phoebe's PPATs addressed students' roles in the classroom and the need to assess their understanding and adapt her instruction.

Dominant forms of knowledge. Forms of teacher knowledge served as internally constructed contextual elements that had a significant impact on the ability for teachers to translate espoused theories into practice which, in turn, affected their tendencies toward learner-centered instruction and the use of formative assessment. Although all teachers rely on folk pedagogy at times and hold forms of propositional knowledge, the primary forms of knowledge that guided Phoebe's assessment practices were theoretical and strategic, rather than propositional. Furthermore, while folk pedagogy informed both Mary and Monica's practice to a significant extent, Monica was actively gaining and applying theoretical knowledge as she grew in her profession.

Constraining contextual elements. Many factors kept teachers in this study from designing learner-centered environments and implementing formative assessment strategies. For Mary and Monica, maxims based on folk pedagogy and cultural norms connected with traditional modes of instruction tended to limit their abilities to apply theoretical and strategic knowledge as well as use reflection, analogical reasoning, and informed judgment in making instructional decisions concerning the assessment of students.

All three teachers struggled with the pressure they felt to cover all of the state-mandated objectives, both in scope and pacing. However, Mary and Monica overtly responded to this pressure to "teach to the test" while Phoebe did not. The belief that students could be successful on the high-stakes exam if they were able to recall declarative knowledge had a significant influence on Mary and Monica's instructional decisions and practices, which resulted in an emphasis on summative assessments, with little emphasis or instructional time for formative assessment practices. Cultural norms of the school and of students also influenced practice. Uniquely identified by Phoebe was her students' resistance to learner-centered instruction due to their personal experiences, habits, and expectations. Monica tended to conform to traditions of science teaching, enacting what she perceived as the expectations of her department and school. Additionally, she struggled with overcoming her experiences as a learner in traditional science classrooms as she attempted to transform her espoused theories into reform-based practices. Mary, on the other hand, was constrained by her beliefs about students' abilities, motivation, and effort and her mental model of how students learn.

Facilitating contextual elements. Phoebe's mental model of how students learn caused her to teach in a manner that empowered students as she shared the responsibility of learning with them. She believed that students construct knowledge through experiences, and she provided those opportunities to the best of her ability. Then she enacted PCI to determine if her approach worked and continually adjusted her instruction in response. Phoebe also felt that her school culture was one that was supportive and collegial, resulting in a sense of autonomy. Monica expressed the same sense of autonomy and enacted PCI as her repertoire of classroom strategies further developed. Mary's content knowledge was her strength, and it served to both hinder (as she imparted it to students) and facilitate (as she used it to find out what students knew) her classroom practice.

Conclusion

These case studies provide an in-depth look at teachers and the factors that influence their decision making. As is evident, deeply held beliefs about learners and learning manifest themselves into practice and therefore impact what goes on in the classroom and consequently what and how students learn. In order to affect change, we are therefore compelled to not only invest in classroom teachers and address their beliefs about learners and learning, but also foster an environment that is conducive to change in an effort to cultivate growth from propositional to strategic knowledge.

Works Cited

Battista, M. T. (1994). Teachers beliefs and the reform movement in mathematics education. *Phi Delta Kappan, 75*(6), 462.

Box, C., Dabbs, J., & Skoog, G. (2015). A case study of teacher personal practice assessment theories and complexities of implementing formative assessment. *American Educational Research Journal – Teaching, Learning and Human Development, 52*(5), 956–983.

Box, M. C. (2008). *Formative assessment: Patterns, personal practice assessment theories, and impact on student achievement and motivation in science* (PhD dissertation), Texas Tech University, Lubbock, TX.

Bransford, J. D., Brown, A. L., & Cocking, R. R. (Eds.). (2000). *How people learn: Brain, mind, experience, and school*. Washington, DC: The National Academies Press.

Cannings, T., & Stager, G. (2003). *Online constructionism and the future of teacher education*. IFIP Working Groups 3.1 and 3.3 Working Conference: ICT and the Teacher of the Future, St. Hilda's College, The University of Melbourne, Australia, Australian Computer Society, Inc.

Clandinin, D. J., & Connelly, F. M. (1996). Teachers' professional knowledge landscapes: Teacher stories. Stories of teachers. School stories. Stories of schools. *Educational Researcher, 25*(3), 24–30.

Coleman, J. S. (1966). *Equality of educational opportunity*. Washington, DC: U.S. Department of Health, Education, and Welfare; Office of Education.

Cornett, J. W. (1990). Utilizing action research in graduate curriculum courses. *Theory into Practice, 29*(3), 185.

Cornett, J. W., Yeotis, C., & Terwilliger, L. (1990). Teacher personal practice theories and their influences upon teacher curricular and instructional actions: A case study of a secondary science teacher. *Science Education, 74*(5), 517–529.

Cuban, L. (1990). Reforming again, again, and again. *Educational Researcher, 19*(1), 3–13.

Czerniak, C. M., Lumpe, A. T., & Haney, J. J. (1999). Science teachers' beliefs and intentions to implement thematic units. *Journal of Science Teacher Education, 10*(2), 123–145.

Darling-Hammond, L. (2000). Teacher quality and student achievement: A review of state policy evidence. *Education Policy Analysis Archives, 8*, 1.

Duschl, R., Schweingruber, H., & Shouse, A. (Eds.). (2007). *Taking science to school: Learning and teaching science in grades K-8*. Washington, DC: The National Academies Press.

Enyedy, N., Goldberg, J., & Welsh, K. M. (2005). Complex dilemmas of identity and practice. *Science Education, 90*(1), 68–93.

Feldman, A. (2000). Decision making in the practical domain: A model of practical conceptual change. *Science Education, 84*(5), 606–623.

Fishman, B. J., & Davis, E. A. (2006). Teacher learning research and the learning sciences. In R. K. Sawyer (Ed.), *The Cambridge handbook of the learning sciences* (pp. 535–550). Cambridge: Cambridge University Press.

Frohbieter, G., Greenwald, E., Stecher, B., & Schwartz, H. (2011). *Knowing and doing: What teachers learn from formative assessment and how they use the information*. CRESST report 802. Retrieved from https://eric.ed.gov/?id=ED522825

Gess-Newsome, J., Southerland, S. A., Johnston, A., & Woodbury, S. (2003). Educational reform, personal practical theories, and dissatisfaction: The anatomy of change in college science teaching. *American Educational Research Journal, 40*(3), 731–767.

Glesne, C. (2006). *Becoming qualitative researchers*. Boston: Pearson.

Goldhaber, D. A. N. (2016). In schools, teacher quality matters most. *Education Next, 16*(2), 56–62.

Gregoire, M. (2003). Is it a challenge or a threat? A dual-process model of teachers' cognition and appraisal processes during conceptual change. *Educational Psychology Review, 15*(2), 147.

Hand, B., Treagust, D., & Vance, K. (1997). Student perceptions of the social constructivist classroom. *Science Education, 81*(5), 561–575.

Ilić, M., & Bojović, Ž. (2016). Teachers' folk pedagogies. *Journal of Arts and Humanities, 5*(9), 41–52.

Jordan, A., & Stanovich, P. (2003). Teachers' personal epistemological beliefs about students with disabilities as indicators of effective teaching practices. *Journal of Research in Special Educational Needs, 3*(1), 1–14.

Levin, B., & Ye, H. (2008). Investigating the content and sources of teacher candidates' personal practical theories (PPTs). *Journal of Teacher Education, 59*(1), 55–68.

McGrath, C., Barman, L., Stenfors-Hayes, T., Roxå, T., Silén, C., & Laksov, K. B. (2016). The ebb and flow of educational change: Change agents as negotiators of change. *Teaching & Learning Inquiry, 4*(2), 1–14.

Nathan, M. J., & Sawyer, R. K. (2014). Foundations of the learning sciences. In R. K. Sawyer (Ed.), *The Cambridge handbook of the learning sciences* (2nd ed., pp. 21–41). New York, NY: Cambridge University Press.

Nye, B., Konstantopoulos, S., & Hedges, L. V. (2004). How large are teacher effects? *Educational Evaluation & Policy Analysis, 26*(3), 237–257.

Orit Avidov, U., & Tamar, S.-I. (2017). ICT coordinators' TPACK-based leadership knowledge in their roles as agents of change. *Journal of Information Technology Education: Research, 16*, 169–188.

Proper, H., Wideen, M., & Ivany, G. (1988). World view projected by science teachers: A study of classroom dialogue. *Science Education, 72*, 547–560.

Rimm-Kaufman, S. E., Storm, M. D., Sawyer, B. E., Pianta, R. C., & LaParo, K. M. (2006). The teacher belief q-sort: A measure of teachers' priorities in relation to disciplinary practices, teaching practices, and beliefs about children. *Journal of School Psychology, 44*(2), 141–165.

Rivers, J. C., & Sanders, W. L. (2002). Teacher quality and equity in educational opportunity: Findings and policy implications. *Teacher Quality*, 13–23.

Sanders, D. P., & McCutcheon, G. (1986). The development of practical theories of teaching. *Journal of Curriculum and Supervision, 2*(1), 50–67.

Schoenfeld, A. H. (2011). *How we think: A theory of goal-oriented decision making and its educational applications.* New York: Routledge.

Shulman, L. (1986). Those who understand: Knowledge growth in teaching. *Educational Researcher, 15*(2), 4–14.

Smith, L. K., & Southerland, S. A. (2007). Reforming practice or modifying reforms?: Elementary teachers' response to the tools of reform. *Journal of Research in Science Teaching, 44*(3), 396–423.

Sweeney, A. E., Bula, O. A., & Cornett, J. W. (2001). The role of personal practice theories in the professional development of a beginning high school chemistry teacher. *Journal of Research in Science Teaching, 38*(4), 408–441.

Wiliam, D., & Leahy, S. (2006, April 6–12). *A theoretical foundation for formative assessment.* Paper presented at the American Educational Research Association (AERA), San Francisco, CA.

CHAPTER 5

The Professional Development of Teachers

As we have seen, the classroom teacher is critical to the success of the entire enterprise of education. This chapter will provide a brief synopsis of past and present credentialing practices and common professional development (PD) programs conducted in the United States and their influence on teachers and in shaping classroom practice. I contend that while our current direction for PD holds promise, it falls short of its potential in light of new findings in the cognitive sciences, the learning needs of twenty-first-century students, and the evolving role of the classroom teacher.

A Brief History

Teacher preparation and credentialing. During the Colonial Period before separating from Great Britain, US education focused on religion, reading, writing, and mathematics—the knowledge and skills that children needed to prosper in the new economy and to live a pious life. It was not surprising that religion was part of the curriculum as colonists were accustomed to their schools being heavily influenced by the Church of England before immigrating to the new world. Teachers were expected to be of high moral character and religious in nature, but little thought was given to their content knowledge or pedagogical practices; moreover, there were no training or certification requirements, although teachers often had to meet the approval of local ministers (Angus, 2001). After the United States separated from Great Britain, formal schooling added civic duty, or

© The Author(s) 2019
C. Box, *Formative Assessment in United States Classrooms*,
https://doi.org/10.1007/978-3-030-03092-6_5

patriotism, to the curriculum. As the United States exerted its independence and created a secular state, "... authority for licensing teachers passed from ecclesiastical to civil authorities, the criteria for licensing expanded to include, first, knowledge of subject matter and later, knowledge of pedagogy, usually determined by means of an examination" (Angus, 2001, p. 13). Training requirements remained inconsistent for classroom teachers, or "schoolmasters" as they were called, until the 1830s when "normal" schools of education were born, concurrent with the emergence of the pre-college common school. These two-year institutes were established to train elementary teachers, who themselves may or may not have completed high school or even grammar school. Normal schools provided the equivalent of high school academics or lower-division college courses and eventually, if they survived, became teacher-training colleges.

By the turn of the century, state-supported women's colleges were formed such as the College of Industrial Arts in Denton, Texas (originally named the Texas Industrial Institute and College for the Education of White Girls of the State of Texas in the Arts and Sciences in 1902, then the Girls Industrial College in 1903). The purpose of such institutes was to provide vocational training to rural and small-town women. Since many areas still lacked comprehensive high schools, students could enroll without a high school diploma and work toward a temporary two-year certificate—the equivalent of a high school degree. Students could then complete further training and earn a 4-year, permanent certificate. Students were awarded a temporary certificate for completion of the coursework and were allowed to be employed during the academic year while working on permanent certification during the summers or through the use of correspondence courses. See Illustration 5.1. This illustration is a snapshot of a job application of a young woman (my paternal grandmother) in Texas submitted in pursuit of employment during World War II. Notice that she had only completed the 11th grade, then gained a 2-year temporary certificate (see Illustration 5.2), and attended school part time during the summer months to gain her 4-year certificate. In order to obtain her temporary certificate, she was required to show proficiency in arithmetic, geography, grammar, history, physiology and hygiene, reading, school law and management, and writing, plus two of the four optional areas including agriculture, composition, drawing, or music. See Illustration 5.3. She attended school while teaching grades 1–7 in a one-room school in a rural, Texas town. She left teaching upon her marriage as was the custom (or a regulation, depending on the area) of the time.

12. Give in the blanks below information regarding your education, including dates:
(a) Grammar school, Attended from _9 1 0_, 1___, to _1 9_ 1 9 1 7.
Higest school year completed _8_

(b) High school, Name and Location _Pleasant Grove Jack Co Tex_
Attended from _9_ 1 9 1 7, to _19 3 0_, .
Highest school year completed _11_ . Were you graduated? _No_
(c)

College or University (Name and location)	Dates attended		Semester Hours Credit	Major Subject		Degree Received	Date of Degree
	From	To		Name	Sem. Hrs.		
C.I.A. Denton Tex	1920	1921				2 Yr Teachers Certificate	
North Tex State Teachers College Denton, Tex	1921	—				4 Yrs Teachers Certificate	

(d) State whether attendance at each school or college was part-time or full-time, and whether at day or evening classes. _part time_

Illustration 5.1 Job application denoting 2- and 4-year certificates

As you can see, teacher training and credentialing were becoming part of the landscape, but Cuban (1993, p. 31) asserted that in order to staff burgeoning classrooms, the most pressing concern of the times was simply to find teachers who were willing to work and who would stay. Therefore, those hired were often inadequately prepared, and irrespective of their lack of training were regularly required to cover up to ten different subjects on a daily basis amid their many other classroom duties.

Secondary school teachers were called upon to teach many upper-level subjects, and the curriculum was geared toward college preparation, making it essential for the teachers themselves to have an education beyond high school. By the late 1890s in New England and New York, over 50% of the teachers were either college graduates or had completed coursework from formal teacher-training schools. "The rapid growth of the recognition of professional and academic study as preparation for teaching is shown by the fact that by 1897, 28 states certified teachers on the basis of graduation from a normal school or university without further examination" (Cook, 1921, p. 12). Rural schools, on the other hand, had difficulty attracting

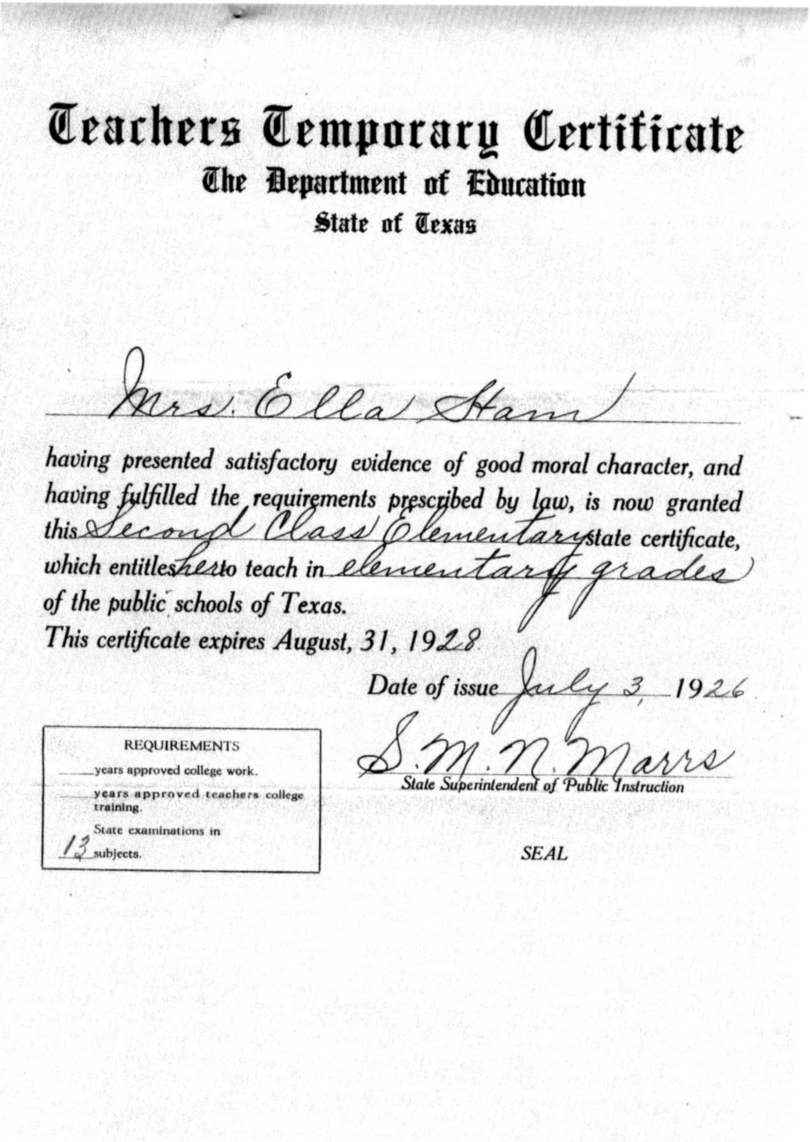

Teachers Temporary Certificate
The Department of Education
State of Texas

_____ Mrs. Ella Ham _____

having presented satisfactory evidence of good moral character, and having fulfilled the requirements prescribed by law, is now granted this *Second Class Elementary* state certificate, which entitles *her* to teach in *elementary grades* of the public schools of Texas.

This certificate expires August, 31, 1928.

Date of issue *July 3, 1926*

S. M. N. Marrs
State Superintendent of Public Instruction

REQUIREMENTS
___ years approved college work.
___ years approved teachers college training.
13 State examinations in subjects.

SEAL

Illustration 5.2 Texas 2-year teaching certificate

THE PROFESSIONAL DEVELOPMENT OF TEACHERS   109

Mrs. Ella Ham

Denton, Texas

R. F. D. .... Box .... Street *1806 W. Mulberry St*

The following is the report of the State Board of Examiners upon your examination papers submitted from .... *Denton* .... County:

ELEMENTARY CERTIFICATE OF THE SECOND CLASS PRESCRIBED		HIGH SCHOOL CERTIFICATE OF THE SECOND CLASS PRESCRIBED	
Arithmetic	78	Civil Government	
Geography, Descriptive	66	Composition, Higher	
Grammar, Elementary	78	Psychology	
History of Texas	74	OPTIONAL Any four of the seven:	
History of United States	71		
Physiology and Hygiene	79	Algebra	
Reading	75	Botany	
School Law	82	Geography, Physical	
School Management	62	Geometry, Plane	
Spelling	90	History, Ancient	
Writing	92	History, Modern	
OPTIONAL Any two of the four:		Literature, American	
Agriculture	66	Total of the twenty High School Second Class Subjects	
Composition, Elementary	85	Average of the twenty High School Second Class Subjects	
Drawing			
Music			
Total of the thirteen Elementary Second Class Subjects	988		
Average of the thirteen Elementary Second Class Subjects	77		

Each applicant receiving a certificate has made not less than 50 in any subject. For a two-years' certificate, each has made an average of not less than 75; for a three-years' certificate, an average of not less than 85. The minimum total for an elementary certificate is 969, for a High School 1490.

READ THIS CAREFULLY

Our estimates of value are recorded on all answers and papers; and before the reports are sent out, the examiners make a careful revision of the papers of every applicant whose general average would indicate that he might be entitled to a certificate. A faithful effort is made to resolve all reasonable doubts in favor of the applicant.

Each applicant should be sure to preserve all examination reports until the building process has been completed to his satisfaction.

Such applicant should, as soon thereafter as practicable, return his elementary certificate upon which he is building, together with all examination reports attached, to the State Department of Education for the high school certificate.

The applicant may take any of the High School subjects as many times as desired, and the highest grade on any subject will be counted in the compiled or final report.

We, therefore, are recommending to the State Superintendent of Public Instruction that a..... *elementary* ..... certificate, valid for a period of *2* ....

Illustration 5.3   Texas 2-year certification exam report

certified teachers, and legislators were reluctant to invest in training teachers to teach in rural schools. As a result, "teacher institutes" were offered by the local counties instead. These teacher institutes were organized by county superintendents who provided summer classes or short courses during the school year. Teachers were then awarded a certificate for passing the county exam. According to Angus (2001, p. 8), most rural school teachers, especially in Midwestern states, either had no training at all or had minimal training through these county teacher institutes.

The formalization of teacher training. As Taylorism flourished during the Progressive Era, so did the formal training and preparation of teachers. "Taylorism complemented the social efficiency thinking of educators because it mandated that workers be scientifically selected and trained for their particular jobs ..." (Spring, 2001, p. 293). By the mid-1900s, both normal schools and rural teacher institutes were a thing of the past, and most teacher-training programs had evolved into four-year courses of study within universities for both elementary and secondary teachers. Teacher candidates were required to have completed high school in order to be admitted. Furthermore, state departments of education gained control over both rural and urban schools. Curriculum in public schools continued to shift its focus away from civic duty, religion, and vocational skills toward an emphasis on formal academics, college preparation, and corporate employment. Likewise, teacher preparation programs (TPPs) began to focus more on academic subjects and student achievement rather than general or vocational education.

In the years that followed, certification requirements varied widely. However, current requirements as outlined under the federally mandated ESSA have become fairly standard even though individual states retain legislating authority in such matters. Currently all public, K-12 teachers, with the exception of some vocational or career preparation positions in select states, are expected to have a teaching certificate (i.e., they have met the minimum standards of competence) and are therefore licensed (i.e., they have been granted legal permission to teach once they have met certification standards) having earned their license from accredited TPPs including undergraduate, graduate, or ACPs. It is important to note, however, that certification requirements do not apply to private institutions and some charter schools. Although teacher certification is required in the public-school setting, teacher shortages have resulted in some schools being forced to hire uncertified teachers under emergency, temporary, or provisional conditions. For example, according to a report published by the

Learning Policy Institute (LPI) (Darling-Hammond, 2018) that evaluated the state of Texas for the 2015–2016 school year, approximately 6.66% of teachers were not fully certified for their teaching assignments (22,791 out of 342,257 teachers), and overall, the LPI estimated that over 100,000 US teachers were not fully certified for their teaching assignments between 2015 and 2017. However, the US Department of Education reported in 2016 that although all states had instances of hiring teachers who were not fully certified, they viewed the overall percentages as small. In 35 states, less than 2% were not fully certified; however, 14 states had schools in which 5% of teachers were not fully certified (U.S. Department of Education-Office of Planning Evaluation and Policy Development-Policy and Program Studies Service, 2016) but were working toward certification.

One response to the teaching shortage has been the rise of ACPs. ACPs allow individuals who already hold a bachelor's degree to enter the classroom without having received formal teacher training from a traditional undergraduate program. In 1983, only 8 states allowed for alternative certification, whereas at the time of this writing, 48 states and the District of Columbia allowed it. According to the US Department of Education's *Schools and Staffing Survey* released in 2016, new hires entering the field of education through alternative certification in 2011–2012 in US public and private schools were estimated at 21.3% (41,748 out of 196,000) and 15% (6525 out of 43,500), respectively (Warner-Griffin, Noel, & Tadler, 2016). The quality and effectiveness of ACPs continue to engender debate, and the discussion is beyond the purpose of this writing. However, a review of the data indicated that AC teachers are more likely than traditionally certified teachers to leave the profession (Redding & Smith, 2016), a negative indicator of their confidence and preparedness to be successful in the complex world of teaching. ACPs place teacher candidates in the classroom without student-teaching experience and often without specialized training in curriculum and instruction, classroom management, educational psychology, assessment, instructional technology, and other foundational competencies that traditional ECPs offer, starting them out underprepared for the challenges that exist. Interestingly, Mary and Monica were both products of an ACP, while Phoebe was not—something to keep in mind as we continue to analyze their success in the classroom.

In brief, licensure and certification requirements vary from program to program and state to state, and the United States is one of the very few developed countries in the world that does not have a uniform federal licensing exam imposed to provide a minimum level of competency by its workforce. The United States has yet to find a system of teacher preparation (or in-service PD for that matter) that is consistent, equitable, and effective. When states exercise autonomy, it is understandable that a myriad of programs exist. However, a variety of programs also means that some are more effective than others.

But as a general rule, most authorities agree that teacher candidates should: (1) have at least a bachelor's degree; some states require a fifth year or master's degree, (2) complete an approved, accredited education program, (3) have a major or minor in education (for elementary education), (4) have a major in the subject area in which they plan to teach (for middle or high school teaching), (5) have a strong liberal-arts foundation, and (6) pass either a state test, the widely used PRAXIS exam, or another exam according to the Educational Policy Institute in Washington, DC (D. Roth & Swail, 2000).

As is evident, the US school system is populated with teachers who vary greatly in foundational knowledge regarding learners and learning, depending on preparation as well as past experiences. Teacher preparation exists on a spectrum. Some teachers enter the classroom with no training whatsoever, others receive quality instruction from four-year universities, and others fall somewhere in between, thrusting each one, regardless of preparedness, into one of the most complex ecosystems in which to work and in which the stakes are high for students and society as a whole.

Training for in-service teachers. Although teacher training in ECPs is of great importance and has the potential to impact teacher quality significantly, especially during the early years of a teacher's tenure, this book focuses on addressing the growth and development of in-service teachers. For additional information on the aims and challenges of initial TPPs, I recommend the National Academy of Education's *Preparing Teachers for a Changing World* (2005) edited by Linda Darling-Hammond and John Bransford.

When looking historically at training for US in-service teachers, in 1892, the Committee of Ten identified the need for more highly qualified teachers and encouraged universities to contribute to their training. Some of the earliest records of PD are described by Cuban in his publication *How Teachers Taught* (1993) that revealed teaching and learning conditions in three school systems between 1920 and 1940: New York, New York, Denver, Colorado, and Washington, DC. These early instances of PD occurred during the Modern Era when schools and teachers were chronically plagued with heavy curricular requirements, time restraints, crowded conditions, and busy schedules. To provide PD opportunities for their teachers, Washington, DC schools brought in professionals from various universities to lecture on topics such as curriculum revision, classroom efficiency, and progressive reading programs. Teachers in this district were also required to attend monthly meetings and listen to lectures on topics such as adapting courses of study to projects and the activity method of teaching. Thus, we are provided with an early example of the ironic practice of employing lecture and direct instruction to educate teachers on constructivist practices such as active and project-based learning. This didactic approach was not surprising given the current climate and conditions of the formal school settings in which they worked. Teachers labored under circumstances that induced and supported instructivist practices while Pestalozzian and Deweyan theories were being promoted by educational reformers, a conflict that continues to this day.

Another recorded example of early in-service training occurred in 1935 in New York City. Benjamin Franklin High School in East Harlem provided training for its teachers to help them develop a better understanding of different cultures (Cuban, 1993, p. 64) at a time when immigration matters overwhelmed the schools and classrooms were not only overcrowded but also culturally diverse. The issue experienced in the 1930s was not unique to that time and place. Rather it is another issue with which we continue to struggle to this day—one of diversity and equity.

Shortly after World War II, teachers who had a 2-year college education were able to participate in continuing education opportunities during the summer months at universities to receive higher graduate degrees. Those summer seminars were fairly popular and exposed a great number of teachers to new knowledge and ideas (Frechtling, Sharp, Carey, & Faden-Kiernan, 1995, p. 2).

The first large-scale training for in-service teachers in the United States occurred as a result of the launching of Sputnik as the nation realized that math and science teachers needed to develop their knowledge and skills in their respective fields in order to keep up with advancements by other countries (Frechtling et al., 1995, p. 3). Funding for PD became abundant and available through the National Science Foundation (NSF) (National Science Foundation, 1994; Wissehr, Concannon, & Barrow, 2011) and was used by researchers and master teachers to develop and field test new science curriculum. Once the new curriculum was developed, PD funding became available, which supported teacher training in content and pedagogy, paid teacher stipends for attendance at summer programs, and payed tuition for graduate credit in the sciences (Wissehr et al., 2011, p. 372). The summer institutes and other trainings provided teachers an opportunity to collaborate and share learning experiences as they worked together toward a common goal of improving instruction—a positive outcome that benefited teachers and students alike. Frechtling claimed, however, that many of these trainings focused more on content and less on pedagogy and pedagogical content knowledge—vital components to successful educational practices.

> Questions were raised about the efficacy of the concepts on which the institutes were modeled, with their emphasis on 'top down' instruction by eminent scientists and their focus on subject matter expertise to the neglect of pedagogic technique and learning theory. There was little concern about implementation of institute precepts in the schools setting in which the teachers functioned, and little evidence that participation had affected teacher behavior and student learning and achievement (p. 4).

Although there was a degree of collaboration and inclusion of classroom teachers in developing some programs, it was the exception, rather than the rule. The top-down delivery approach to PD for teachers, once again, was not surprising given that their mode of PD instruction was influenced by the times just as classrooms were. As a general rule, school systems dealt with a large number of teachers who were given little time to devote to professional growth. Behaviorist theories influenced practice, and the one-size-fits-all mentality that drove classroom instruction was further actualized through both the education of in-service teachers as well as students in the classroom.

Where we are now. Those who have been in the teaching profession in the United States for any length of time are no doubt familiar with the traditional in-service teacher education and training (INSET) model of PD. In 2005, nearly all teachers completed some type of PD (Drury & Baer, 2011, p. 35). According to Drury and Baer, teachers on average completed six 5-hour sessions for the year. Although exceptions exist, as a general rule these workshops were conducted by outside consultants who had content expertise but were not situated within the context of the participants teaching environment. These one-day workshops typically focused on curriculum and instruction in content areas and to a lesser extent (in the Drury study) diversity and data-driven decision making. Often, this type of workshop was delivered through didactic or instructivistic means rather than active or constructivistic ones. In fact, an interim NCLB report issued by the US Department of Education in 2007 claimed that in

2003–2004, "fewer than one in four teachers reported that they often participated in professional development that involved active learning opportunities" (Birman et al., 2007, p. 76), or in other words, most teachers were passive recipients in what is colloquially referred to as "sit and get" sessions. On a positive note, many teachers attended workshops in a concerted effort to improve their craft, but unfortunately, this was not the case across the board. Some teachers participated in these educational opportunities for the sole purpose of earning the required continuing education credits, thereby making them less than willing participants. Wilson and Berne (1999) contended that the teacher lore surrounding traditional in-service programs was that teachers found most sessions irrelevant, boring, sometimes amusing, and often of little worth (p. 174). The NEA reported that in 2006, teachers ranked PD near the bottom of the list of factors that helped them in their efforts to provide the best service in their teaching positions contrary to 1976, when it had ranked at the top (Wolman, 2010, p. 92).

This traditional approach to in-service teacher training is often derisively referred to as "stand-alone," "one-shot," "drive-by," "quick-fix," or "make and take" PD. The terms themselves are indicative of the approach, perceived effectiveness, and level of respect held by teachers. Experts agree. Many educators and educational researchers (Ball, 1999; Borko, 2004; Darling-Hammond & Richardson, 2009; Goldenberg & Gallimore, 1991; Sykes, 1996; Thompson & Goe, 2009) have described traditional PD as superficial, woefully inadequate and a waste of time and money. Gary Sykes (1996) went so far as to write "the phrase 'one-shot workshop' has entered educational parlance as shorthand for superficial, faddish in-service education that supports a mini-industry of consultants without having much effect on what goes on in schools and classrooms" (p. 465), a sad commentary, indeed.

To add insult to injury, the NCLB report (Birman et al., 2007) also cited that in 2004–2005, approximately $1.14 billion was spent on PD in the United States, yet returns have been marginal. Educators have thus begun to acknowledge the problems associated with traditional PD. Reform efforts have emerged, and the landscape of PD is slowly changing. Many influential entities such as the Association for Supervision and Curriculum Development, Educational Testing Service, National Governors' Association, and National Academy of Sciences, Engineering, and Medicine among others promote a more constructivist approach to in-service training and support based on what is now known about how people learn along with effective practices as revealed through research. The US Department of Education (Rotermund, DeRoche, & Ottem, 2017), citing experts in the field such as Linda Darling-Hammond, Laura Desimone, and Michael Garet, provided a summary that reflects current knowledge and a consensus view of effective PD. This report indicated that PD is most effective when it (1) focuses on the content of the subject taught; (2) corresponds with school or classroom activities; (3) provides active learning opportunities (e.g., observing expert teachers or leading discussions); (4) is sustained over time; (5) involves collective participation of teachers from the same school, subject, or grade; and (6) includes administrative support for planning and implementing change (p. 2).

Despite this current perspective however, the verdict is not yet in. Research evaluating the effectiveness of this enhanced approach to PD is in its infancy as the field evolves and stakeholders investigate what high-quality PD looks like, how it is experienced, and what outcomes should be measured. Guskey (2003) analyzed 13 different lists of the characteristics of effective PD, and although they identified similar key features, most used different criteria to determine "effectiveness," making analysis decidedly difficult. Surprisingly, only a small number of research studies connected PD to learning outcomes—our ultimate goal in education.

> The characteristics that influence the effectiveness of professional development are multiple and highly complex. It may be unreasonable, therefore, to assume that a single list of characteristics leading to broadbrush policies and guidelines for effective professional development will ever emerge, regardless of the quality of professional development research. Still, by agreeing on the criteria for "effectiveness" and providing clear descriptions of important contextual elements, we can guarantee sure and steady progress in our efforts to improve the quality of professional development endeavors. (Guskey, 2003, p. 750)

Desimone (2011) addressed concerns posed by Guskey and posited that if we are to accurately measure effectiveness, we must (1) identify key features of effective PD, (2) place them in a conceptual framework of how it works, and then (3) measure the following three outcomes: Do teachers learn? Do they change their practices? And does student achievement increase as a result?

Desimone's key features of effective PD are congruent with other experts in the field and include content focus, active learning, coherence, duration, and collective participation. She proposed a basic model of how successful PD leads to enhanced student learning and claimed that it lays a foundation that informs its effectiveness. According to Desimone, successful PD follows these steps:

1. Teachers experience PD.
2. The PD increases teachers' knowledge and skills, changes their attitudes and beliefs, or both.
3. Teachers use their new knowledge, skills, attitudes, and beliefs to improve the content of their instruction, their approach to pedagogy, or both.
4. The instructional changes that the teachers introduce to the classroom boost students' learning.

The framework is not only simple and straightforward, it also leads to opportunities for measuring outcomes and can be applied to most, if not all, PD initiatives. It is important to note that her steps confer a gain in knowledge and skills with changes in attitudes and beliefs occurring in teachers *before* they apply them in the classroom. Guskey, on the other hand (2002), proposed a model for conceptual change with the assertion that altered beliefs and attitudes do not occur in teachers until after they have implemented new strategies and see positive results from their students. "These improvements typically result from changes teachers have made in their classroom practices—a new instructional approach, the use of new materials or curricula, or simply a modification in teaching procedures or classroom format" (p. 383). Sfard and Cobb (2014) concurred stating that knowledge and beliefs initially held by teachers become refined in the context of practice as they participate in new activities. Thus, conceptual change is predicated on the notion that teachers must be willing to try new things and then honestly evaluate them, reflecting on their levels of success. Chapter 6 provides an analysis of conceptual change in light of the ADM and will reveal that change is rarely a linear process, but rather recursive and fluid.

That being said, it is difficult to ascertain exactly what goes on in PDs across the country; however, in an effort to analyze the content of PDs, a survey conducted by the US Department of Education (Rotermund et al., 2017) reported that the most prevalent topic of teacher PD in 2011–2012 was the content of the subject(s) taught (85%), followed by the use of computers for instruction (67%), reading instruction (57%), student discipline and classroom management (43%), teaching students with disabilities (37%), and teaching ELL/ELP students (27%)—oddly reminiscent of the Washington, DC, programs in the 1920s which provided training in curriculum revision, classroom efficiency, and progressive reading instruction.

These PD topics are relevant and useful to teachers and schools alike and are typically presented as a hybrid of content, pedagogy, and strategy implementation. Yet I contend that we are neglecting the underlying constructs which exert a tremendous influence over whether or not the strategies presented become embedded in teacher practices and to what degree that occurs. Additionally, I believe that we are overlooking the impact that the twenty-first century has or should have on both teaching and student learning.

Underlying Constructs

Refer back to the ADM in Chap. 4 (Fig. 4.2) to put PD in context. In a traditional PD setting where the topic is formative assessment, the training would typically emphasize (1) the purpose and focus of assessment—in this case providing teachers with particular assessment strategies to use in classrooms. However, teachers may be left on their own without guidance, support, or feedback to (2) plan how and when to use assessment, (3) develop the knowledge needed to implement assessment practices with fidelity, and (4) reflect on the effectiveness of their practice and adjust their teaching accordingly. This ineffective approach to PD is destined for failure as with any other one-shot PD session. Even ongoing, sustained PD using the criteria promoted by the US Department of Education may still fall short of effecting change to a substantial degree. We are remiss if we do not purposefully and explicitly address (5) the underlying constructs that determine a teacher's PPATs such as the mental model of how students learn, their own implicit theories of intelligence, and the forms of knowledge they employ, and (6) the externally imposed contextual elements over which we have a measure of control, such as student mindsets, metacognitive skills, and learning expectations for students. Addressing these constructs has the potential to change teachers' conceptions of their role as a teacher, and thus the likelihood of enhancing their assessment practices to a degree that empowers students and makes inroads to improved student achievement.

In the following paragraphs, we will investigate those constructs and set the stage for thinking about how they can be purposefully addressed in teacher development programs.

Mental model of how students learn. Mary's (and all teachers for that matter) mental model of how students learn affected her practice in significant ways. She believed that students learned by listening, memorizing, and repeating. She had an abundance of content knowledge, was a master at classroom management, knew how to use technology, and was not prone to use new strategies (the topic of most PDs), thus making traditional PD opportunities of little use to her. Mary was not alone in her approach to teaching. The legacy of lecture still prevails in many secondary science classrooms, continuing the tradition passed on by faculty in higher education. According to a recent survey (Stains et al., 2018), 55% of STEM (Science, Technology, Engineering, and Math) faculty still use lecture as a primary means of teaching in undergraduate courses at the college level, and we know that the path of least resistance for teachers is to teach in the same manner under which they learned. As a result, this adherence to traditions creates a cycle that is difficult to break.

Additionally, Mary held a belief about her pre-advanced placement and on-level students' abilities to learn and was convinced that students were either intelligent or they were not. She had low expectations for and little faith in her on-level students, indicators of an entity rather than incremental theory of intelligence. A long history of research has revealed the idea of a "self-fulfilling prophesy," and that students will, indeed, live up (or down) to a teacher's expectations. In a recent study on teacher mindsets and how they translate into practice, Rattan, Good, and Dweck (2012) discovered that teachers (specifically mathematics teachers in this case) who construed intelligence as fixed (1) quickly diagnosed students as having low ability based on a single poor performance, (2) orchestrated classroom practices that inadvertently reduced engagement, and (3) directly reported that they did not expect much improvement from their students (p. 736). A teacher's mental model of how students learn and hence his or her beliefs about learners had a profound effect on instruction.

> Similarly, the expectations a teacher has for his or her students, based on their beliefs about students as learners, has the greatest impact in the classroom. Even if unspoken, it seems that the teacher's beliefs about a student are communicated; teacher expectations affect the student's self-concept as a learner, which in turn influences student approaches to learning (citing Trouiloud et al., 2002, 2006 in Hohnen & Murphy, 2016).

Schoenfeld used the term *orientations* to describe a teacher's beliefs, dispositions, values, tastes, and preferences, citing that orientations shape what people perceive and interpret. In his book *How We Think* (2011), he described how it may be possible to catalyze orientational shifts by exposing teachers to the idea that orientation determines one's practices and inducing teachers to reflect on their own orientations. Likewise, the same could be said about mindsets. How would a teacher with an entity theory of intelligence change their behavior if that teacher understood the consequences of his or her beliefs, and that those beliefs were in error? How might they change their approach to teaching if they had a solid understanding of the anatomy and physiology of the brain and the structural changes that occur in the brain during learning events? This area of research is ripe with possibilities and has yet to be explored, and the findings have the potential to have significant implications for students, educators, and researchers alike.

Although little research has been conducted to date on how a teacher's mental model of learning might change as a result of examining the neuroscience behind learning, much research has been conducted in the fields of neuro- and cognitive science about neuroplasticity—the concept that underlies theories of intelligence. Recall that research findings revealed that the brain is indeed very malleable and changes over time (Fitzgerald & Laurian-Fitzgerald, 2016; Sousa, 2006), supporting the incremental theory of intelligence (as opposed to the entity theory of intelligence as fixed) which is critical to understanding learners and learning. Simply put, the brain changes its structure and function in response to experiences as it adapts to its environment. "Every time we carry out an action, a cell fires, and changes become wired into the brain and are strengthened when cells are simultaneously activated many times. This action causes neural circuits to form in the brain. The stronger the circuit, the greater the skill" (Hohnen & Murphy, 2016, p. 76). Many research studies have shown that teaching students about the brain and how it changes during learning has tremendous potential to move them from an entity to an incremental theory of intelligence (see Aronson, Fried, & Good, 2002; Blackwell, Trzesniewski, & Dweck, 2007; Dweck, 2006). Although there exists a lack of research on the topic, logic would suggest that the same must hold true for teachers as well. Modern research about the brain, then, provides a scientific basis for what we believe to be true about the potential of both our teachers and our students to grow and learn. "What we find is people really do change their brain functions in response to experience," said Kurt W. Fischer, the director of Harvard University's Mind, Brain, and Education Program. "It's just amazing how flexible the brain is. That plasticity has been a huge surprise to a whole lot of people" (Sparks, 2012).

Such insights into the science of learning have enormous potential to shape the attitudes and behaviors of both teachers and students in effect leaving us negligent if we fail to expose teachers (pre-service as well as in-service) to the science of learning and the implications for our students as a result. However, an important caveat to note here: the neuroscience of learning is in its infancy, and we must be cautious as we link findings to classroom practice. Historically, premature and hasty responses to studies concerning the brain have resulted in neuromyths about learning such as the left-brain, right-brain assignment claiming that the left hemisphere is the seat of language and rational thinking, while the right hemisphere is responsible for intuition, emotion, and the non-verbal and synthetic thinking required for spatial tasks (Weigmann, 2013). This conclusion turned out to be an oversimplification and misguided application of research findings on hemispheric differences conducted on epilepsy patients in the 1960s. This and other myths have been based on the misinterpretation of valid scientific results that needed more time and analysis before applying their findings to learning, learners, and classroom practice. However,

> The list of conclusions that cannot be drawn from neuroscience is long, but this does not preclude that neuroscience can contribute to education. There are promising approaches to unravelling brain functions that are directly relevant to school education, and considerable progress has been made in understanding the neurocognitive underpinning of essential skills such as reading and calculating. In these areas, neuroscience and cognitive psychology have teamed up to elucidate the learning process and re-paving the way towards classroom application. (Weigmann, 2013, p. 137)

Conceptual change in teachers. Consequently, the question remains: does PD have the potential to create conceptual change in a teacher's mental model of learning? In a recent study by Wilson, Sztajn, Edgington, Webb, and Myers (2017), the researchers examined teacher discourse in a PD setting to determine if they could detect a change in teachers' thinking about student learning as a result of PD efforts focused on learning trajectories. Learning trajectory-based instruction is founded on the theory that students have a path by which learning might proceed from their own starting point to an intended learning goal that is not always linear, but it is also not random. Trajectories "represent ordered expected tendencies developed through empirical research designed to identify highly probable steps students follow as they develop their initial mathematical ideas into formal concepts, recognizing that each student's path can be unique" (Sztajn,

Confrey, Wilson, & Edgington, 2012, p. 147). Thus, it pays attention to how students learn rather than focusing on knowledge of the discipline, which is the typical approach. The researchers claimed that "learning about student thinking leads to increased instructional agency because teachers generate new meanings for students' academic successes and struggles in professional discussions" (p. 570) and that a teacher's mental model of learning (they termed "frameworks for student thinking") is revealed through professional discourse. Their study resulted in findings that revealed to what extent their intervention worked and to what extent it fell short. Findings indicated that teachers who were trained in learning trajectory-based instruction were more likely to consider prior knowledge and experiences when discussing student thinking, but there was little change in their "ability storylines" about students, one of the stated goals of the training. Teachers further continued to use a narrative that implied ability as innate using terms such as "high" and "low" students, subsequently neglecting to realize an incremental theory of intelligence related to the learning trajectories that the PD leaders sought to instill.

> As a consequence, we suggest that by themselves, broad guidelines and implicit expectations for professional development discussions focused on student thinking are insufficient to challenge deeply rooted ideas about ability. We propose that more explicit and targeted attention is needed to transform the narrative that innate ability determines students' academic performance. (P. H. Wilson et al., 2017, p. 598)

Although the study is small and in a single school which limits its generalizability, the findings indicated that PD efforts that seek to target a teacher's mental model of learning must be explicit and more direct in order to address and perhaps alter a teacher's implicit theories of intelligence.

Developing theoretical and strategic knowledge. Teacher knowledge is an additional underlying construct that influences a teacher's PPATs and therefore what goes on in the classroom. Shulman introduced the terms propositional, case or theoretical, and strategic knowledge in his 1986 publication *Those who understand: Knowledge growth in teaching* (L. S. Shulman, 1986) along with his description of content, pedagogical, and pedagogical content knowledge. The latter terms have become well-known and taken their place as common vernacular in the world of education, and rightfully so. The former are less familiar and get lost among other commonly used terms related to teacher knowledge including explicit (known and communicable) and tacit knowledge (skills, ideas, and experiences that are not easy to communicate); declarative (having knowledge *of* something), procedural (can be used and is acquired by doing), and conceptual knowledge (reflects an understanding); professional knowledge for teaching (public, community-generated, and subject to evaluation); and practitioner knowledge (personal, local, and hard to verify) among many others—the list is long and varied. This study focused on *forms* of content and pedagogical knowledge that, according to Shulman, includes propositional, case or theoretical, and strategic knowledge.

As a reminder, propositional knowledge represents the "what," case or theoretical represents the "how," and strategic knowledge represents the "why" of teaching. All teacher knowledge is important to consider, but our concern is related to the knowledge that teachers need in order to effectively implement reform practices into their curricular routines. Propositional knowledge characterized by folk pedagogy is a given (regardless of the extent of teacher preparation and experience) and is insufficient in navigating the complexities of providing effective learning environments for students. For this reason, teachers must develop theoretical and strategic knowledge. Theoretical knowledge helps make sense of propositional knowledge in that teachers can translate what they know to be true (whether it's accurate or not) into action in the classroom. It provides a framework, context, and relevant details that should be considered when applying what is known about a given situation and is foundational to the development of strategic knowledge. Both propositional and theoretical knowledge "share the burden of unilaterality, the deficiency of turning the reader or user toward a single, particular rule or practical way of seeing" (p. 12) and hence a limited vision of what to do when conflicting principles arise as they invariably do in the complex world of education.

Shulman described the importance of strategic knowledge held by teachers and noted the significance of coupling that knowledge with ongoing reflection that leads to a metacognitive awareness as teachers apply and further develop strategic knowledge.

> ...critical analysis of one's own practice and critical examination of how well students have responded are central elements of any teaching model. At the heart of that learning is the process of critical reflection. (Shulman & Shulman, 2004, pp. 263–264)

Thus, teachers develop the knowledge and metacognitive skills needed to address the complexity inherent in teaching and learning environments, and continue to grow as learners, themselves.

Learning Outcomes for Twenty-First-Century Learners

In addition to addressing underlying constructs that guide teaching such as mental models of learning and forms of knowledge, a new vision should be cast based on what our students need to know and be able to do within a knowledge economy. Content knowledge in math, science, technology, language arts, and social studies continues to remain a fundamental necessity for students. However, it has become increasingly apparent that twenty-first-century students need more as they prepare for higher education or the workforce. With the advent of technology resulting in an overabundance of information that can be both overwhelming and confusing at times, students need to know how to find, curate, and use the available information accurately and efficiently. Students need to understand how to analyze data and be able to determine its validity and value. They need to be adept at determining *what* they need to know and thus *how* to answer and solve complex problems using higher-level thinking skills. Equally important is the need to foster students' abilities to monitor and regulate their own cognitive behaviors as they navigate learning and apply new knowledge and to develop social and emotional competencies that enable them to work collaboratively with others in a productive manner. See Table 5.1 for a summary of what three leading educational entities, the National Research Council (2013), the National Education Association (2014), and the Organisation for Economic Co-operation and Development (Schleicher, 2012) suggested that students need in a knowledge economy.

The skills listed in Table 5.1 are a bit overwhelming and quite different from traditional learning objectives to which teachers are accustomed. Nevertheless, US students deserve to be adequately prepared for success in the innovation age. In concert with learning the content, they must become self-regulated learners—a feature that historically tends to be a serendipitous result of classroom instruction rather than part of a purposeful plan designed to equip students for their future. As societal needs change along with the wants and needs of its workers, we are obligated to prepare students to prosper in the new economy and that includes addressing their implicit beliefs about their ability to learn, developing higher-order thinking capabilities, and fostering the skills needed to monitor and mediate their own learning in order to be productive and to prosper. Yet we rarely (if ever) make student mindsets and developing metacognitive

Table 5.1 Twenty-first-century competencies, skills, and dimensions for students

NRC's twenty-first-century competencies
Cognitive domain

| Cognitive processes and strategies | Knowledge | Creativity |

Critical thinking, information literacy, reasoning and argumentation, innovation

Intrapersonal domain

| Intellectual openness | Work ethic and conscientiousness | Positive core self-evaluation |

Flexibility, initiative, appreciation for diversity, metacognition (the ability to reflect on one's own learning and make adjustments accordingly)

Interpersonal domain

| Teamwork and collaboration | Leadership |

Communication, collaboration, responsibility, conflict resolution

NEA's twenty-first-century skills
Critical thinking and problem solving
Reason effectively, systems thinking, make judgments and decisions, solve problems

Communication
Communicate clearly, including speaking, listening, using multimedia, in diverse environments

Collaboration
Collaborate with others effectively and respectfully, flexibility, willingness to work, valuing others

Creativity and innovation
Think creatively, work creatively with others, implement innovation

OECD's dimensions of a twenty-first-century education
Knowledge
Real world relevant, significant, and applicable

Skills
Higher-order thinking such as the 4 Cs

Character
Adaptability, persistence, resilience, integrity, justice, empathy, ethics

Meta-layer
Learning how to learn (metacognition), interdisciplinarity, systems thinking, personalization

---

acuity a priority. Instead, we focus on the acquisition of knowledge related to our content, and consequently students are equipped to simply pass through school rather than being prepared to tackle contemporary problems beyond the classroom.

The Role of the Twenty-First-Century Teacher

The narrative above foreshadows the redefined role that teachers should play in the new economy. In the early days of the nation, the teacher's job was to manage the masses and try to find ways to accommodate the large influx of students and prepare them to live in an industrious economy. A changed economy calls for a responsive school system and in effect a newly defined role for the classroom teacher (or rather newly rediscovered). Considering what contemporary students need to know and be able to do reaffirms the vision of teaching that Dewey, the founder of progressive education, promoted many years ago, viewing the teacher as a guide, mentor, or facilitator of learning. Until the advent of technology, the teacher and textbooks were the conduit to information for students, and teachers felt tremendous responsibility to transmit knowledge and skills in their respective areas. But the technology revolution brought with it a new passageway for information, yet many teachers have retained vestigial notions of what it means to teach and what it means for students to learn. The twenty-first century has ushered in a knowledge economy that requires students to be equipped to navigate through it. "An emphasis on what students can do with knowledge, rather than what units of knowledge they have, is the essence of twenty-first-century skills" (Silva, 2009, p. 630), and it is the teacher's job to adjust to new demands and responsibilities.

There is no doubt that teachers are obligated to teach content. Students need a deep factual knowledge base from which to work. Cited as the second key finding in *How People Learn*, the NRC (Bransford et al., 2000, p. 16) suggested that in order for students to develop competence, they must have a deep foundation of factual knowledge that is framed in a way that students can retrieve and use what they have learned in a beneficial way. Historically, we have worked toward teaching and testing factual knowledge but have neglected helping students synthesize information in the context of a conceptual framework and organize it in ways that allow transfer—a higher-order thinking skill. Workers in today's innovation-driven, knowledge economy need those analytical skills more than ever. Therefore, teachers need to shift their thinking from the role of teacher as informer, to teacher as designer, architect, and facilitator of learning whose purpose it is to provide an environment that supports the creation and use of knowledge—a meaningful skill for the twenty-first century and beyond. Developing formative assessment expertise is fundamental to this end as the process lends itself to deepening the content knowledge that students have while simultaneously empowering them in their own learning.

Conclusion

Improvements have been made in our approach to PD over the last few decades as we attempt to match theories of learning with the professional growth of teachers. New recommendations for PD abound and leaders continue to find ways to turn theory into practice within a system that is indisputably unwieldy and not prone to change. As educational leaders contemplate priorities for teacher training, given their time and systemic restraints, it is imperative that they purposefully attend to fundamental constructs that influence decision making rather than simply hoping that teacher beliefs and attitudes change as a result of training efforts. Teachers are agents of change with considerable potential to transform learning opportunities for students, but for many teachers, their personal theories about assessment must change first. The following chapter will address the challenges associated with implementing such ambitious goals and suggest important directional shifts and strategies for extending our knowledge into the new learning frameworks that support them.

Works Cited

Angus, D. L. (2001). *Professionalism and the public good: A brief history of teacher certification.* Washington, DC: Thomas B. Fordham Foundation.

Aronson, J., Fried, C. B., & Good, C. (2002). Reducing the effects of stereotype threat on African American college students by shaping theories of intelligence. *Journal of Experimental Social Psychology, 38*(2), 113–125.

Ball, D. L. (1999). Developing practice, developing practitioners: Toward a practice-based theory of professional education. In *Teaching as the learning profession: Handbook of policy and practice* (pp. 3–32). San Francisco: Jossey Bass.

Birman, B. F., Le Floch, K. C., Klekotka, A., Ludwig, M., Taylor, J., Walters, K., ... Yoon, K.-S. (2007). *State and local implementation of the "No Child Left Behind Act." Volume II—Teacher quality under "NCLB": Interim Report.* US Department of Education.

Blackwell, L. S., Trzesniewski, K. H., & Dweck, C. S. (2007). Implicit theories of intelligence predict achievement across an adolescent transition: A longitudinal study and an intervention. *Child Development, 35*(1), 246–263.

Borko, H. (2004). Professional development and teacher learning: Mapping the terrain. *Educational Researcher, 33*(8), 3–15.

Bransford, J. D., Brown, A. L., & Cocking, R. R. (Eds.). (2000). *How people learn: Brain, mind, experience, and school.* Washington, DC: The National Academies Press.

Cook, K. M. (1921). *State laws and regulations governing teachers certificates.* In (Vol. Bulletin, No. 22): Bureau of Education, Department of the Interior.
Cuban, L. (1993). *How teachers taught: Constancy and change in American classrooms, 1890–1990* (2nd ed.). New York: Teachers College Press.
Darling-Hammond, L. (2018). *Learning Policy Institute.* Retrieved from https://learningpolicyinstitute.org/
Darling-Hammond, L., & Bransford, J. (Eds.). (2005). *Preparing teachers for a changing world: What teachers should learn and be able to do* (1st ed.). San Francisco, CA: Sponsored by the National Academy of Education, Jossey-Bass.
Darling-Hammond, L., & Richardson, N. (2009). Research review/teacher learning: What matters. *Educational Leadership, 66*(5), 46–53.
Desimone, L. M. (2011). A primer on effective professional development. *The Phi Delta Kappan, 92*(6), 68–71.
Drury, D., & Baer, J. (2011). *The American public school teacher: Past, present, and future.* Cambridge, MA: Harvard Education Press.
Dweck, C. S. (2006). *Mindset: The new psychology of success.* New York: Ballantine Books.
Fitzgerald, C. J., & Laurian-Fitzgerald, S. (2016). Helping students enhance their grit and growth mindsets. *Journal Plus Education, 14,* 52–67.
Frechtling, J. A., Sharp, L., Carey, N., & Faden-Kiernan, N. (1995). *Teacher enhancement programs: A perspective on the last four decades.* National Science Foundation Directorate for Education and Human Services.
Goldenberg, C., & Gallimore, R. (1991). Changing teaching takes more than a one-shot workshop. *Educational Leadership, 49*(3), 69–72.
Guskey, T. R. (2002). Professional development and teacher change. *Teachers and Teaching, 8*(3), 381–391.
Guskey, T. R. (2003). What makes professional development effective? *Phi Delta Kappan, 84*(10), 748–750.
Hohnen, B., & Murphy, T. (2016). The optimum context for learning; Drawing on neuroscience to inform best practice in the classroom. *Educational & Child Psychology, 33*(1), 75–90.
National Research Council. (2013). *Education for life and work: Developing transferable knowledge and skills in the 21st century.* Washington, DC: The National Academies Press.
National Science Foundation. (1994). *The National Science Foundation: A brief history.* Retrieved from https://www.nsf.gov/about/history/nsf50/nsf8816.jsp
Preparing 21st century students for a global society: An educator's guide to the "Four Cs". (2014). Retrieved from http://www.nea.org/tools/52217.htm
Rattan, A., Good, C., & Dweck, C. S. (2012). "It's ok—Not everyone can be good at math": Instructors with an entity theory comfort (and demotivate) students. *Journal of Experimental Social Psychology, 48*(3), 731–737.

Redding, C., & Smith, T. M. (2016). Easy in, easy out: Are alternatively certified teachers turning over at increased rates? *American Educational Research Journal, 53*(4), 1086–1125.

Rotermund, S., DeRoche, J., & Ottem, R. (2017). *Teacher professional development by selected teacher and school characteristics: 2011–12.* Stats in Brief. NCES 2017-200. National Center for Education Statistics.

Roth, D., & Swail, W. S. (2000). *Certification and teacher preparation in the United States.* Washington, DC. Retrieved from www.educationalpolicy.org

Schleicher, A. (Ed.). (2012). *Preparing teachers and developing school leaders for the 21st Century: Lessons from around the world.* OECD Publishing.

Schoenfeld, A. H. (2011). *How we think: A theory of goal-oriented decision making and its educational applications.* New York: Routledge.

Sfard, A., & Cobb, P. (2014). Research in mathematics education: What can it teach us about human learning. In *The Cambridge handbook of the learning sciences* (pp. 545–563). Cambridge, UK: Cambridge University Press.

Shulman, L. S. (1986). Those who understand: Knowledge growth in teaching. *Educational Researcher, 15*(2), 4–14.

Shulman, L. S., & Shulman, J. H. (2004). How and what teachers learn: A shifting perspective. *Journal of Curriculum Studies, 36*(2), 257–271.

Silva, E. (2009). Measuring skills for 21st-century learning. *Phi Delta Kappan, 90*(9), 630–634.

Sousa, D. A. (2006). *How the brain learns* (3rd ed.). Thousand Oaks, CA: Corwin Press.

Sparks, S. (2012). Neuroscientists find learning is not 'hard-wired'. *Education Week, 31*(33), 16–17.

Spring, J. H. (2001). *The American school, 1642–2000* (5th ed.). Boston: McGraw-Hill.

Stains, M., Harshman, J., Barker, M. K., Chasteen, S. V., Cole, R., DeChenne-Peters, S. E., ... Rodela, T. M. (2018). Anatomy of STEM teaching in North American universities. *Science, 359*(6383), 1468–1470.

Sykes, G. (1996). Reform of and as professional development. *The Phi Delta Kappan, 77*(7), 464–467.

Sztajn, P., Confrey, J., Wilson, P. H., & Edgington, C. (2012). Learning trajectory based instruction: Toward a theory of teaching. *Educational Researcher, 41*(5), 147–156.

Thompson, M., & Goe, L. (2009). *Models for effective and scalable teacher professional development.* Retrieved from http://www.ets.org/Media/Research/pdf/RR-09-07.pdf

U.S. Department of Education-Office of Planning Evaluation and Policy Development-Policy and Program Studies Service. (2016). *Prevalence of teachers without full state certification and variation across schools and states.* Washington, DC.

Warner-Griffin, C., Noel, A., & Tadler, C. (2016). *Sources of newly hired teachers in the United States: Results from the schools and staffing survey, 1987–88 to 2011–12.* NCES 2016-876. Retrieved from https://files.eric.ed.gov/fulltext/ED569202.pdf

Weigmann, K. (2013). Educating the brain. The growing knowledge about how our brain works can inform educational programmes and approaches, in particular, for children with learning problems. *EMBO Reports, 14*(2), 136–139.

Wilson, S. M., & Berne, J. (1999). Teacher learning and the acquisition of professional knowledge: An examination of research on contemporary professional development. *Review of Research In Education, American Educational Research Association, 24*(1), 173–209.

Wilson, P. H., Sztajn, P., Edgington, C., Webb, J., & Myers, M. (2017). Changes in teachers' discourse about students in a professional development on learning trajectories. *American Educational Research Journal, 54*(3), 568–604.

Wissehr, C., Concannon, J., & Barrow, L. H. (2011). Looking back at the Sputnik era and its impact on science education. *School Science and Mathematics, 111*(7), 368–375.

Wolman, P. (2010). *Status of the American public school teacher, 2005–2006.* National Education Association Research Department.

CHAPTER 6

A Renewed Vision for Professional Development

This chapter provides a renewed vision for professional development that builds on current models and is grounded in the learning sciences, suggesting design elements including Wiggins and McTighe's backward design as a framework for planning, and Chappuis' *Seven Strategies of Assessment for Learning* to help teachers achieve their professional goals. Popham (2008) contended that formative assessment has the potential to be *transformative* in that "classroom assessment can fundamentally transform the way a teacher teaches" (p. vii). For formative assessment practices (or any reform practices for that matter) to become transformative, teachers must be involved in professional development opportunities that provide the structure, experiences, and support to help them change their beliefs, increase their knowledge, and alter their habits (Box, 2008; Loucks-Horsley, Love, Stiles, Mundry, & Hewson, 2003). This chapter provides a rationale and suggestions for change in teacher learning that can build teacher capacity, equipping them to meet the needs of twenty-first-century learners. Our purpose here is to support the growth of teachers as they learn to engineer, implement, and maintain constructivist learning environments in which formative assessment is seamlessly embedded as they work to empower students in their own learning.

Teacher Learning

The changing landscape of teacher learning is slow yet promising. Although a difficult task, it is indeed possible to effect positive change in teacher practice, a condition necessary for reform. The serendipitous nature of teacher learning makes it challenging, however, to pinpoint events that have the most influence on what teachers know and can do. Teachers learn informally from casual conversations with colleagues, parents, students, or administrators; from observing their colleagues teach; from publications, blogs, social media, webinars, and online interactions with Professional Learning Networks (PLNs); or from everyday trial and error in their own classrooms. They learn more formally from participation in local, state, and national conferences, one-shot INSET workshops, Professional Learning Communities (PLCs) at their schools or within their districts, school-organized book studies, graduate schools, mentoring programs, new-teacher academies, involvement with universities, consortium or grant initiatives, and more recently, with educative curriculum materials (for a thorough description of educative curriculum materials, see Davis, Palincsar, Smith, Arias, & Kademian, 2017). But the bottom line is this: teachers need to know what to do and how to do it within the contextual complexity of real classrooms. Never before has the demand on teachers been greater and the system in which they work more complex. Darling-Hammond and Bransford (2005) summed it up by stating that

> Standards for learning are now higher than they have ever been before, as citizens and workers need greater knowledge and skill to survive and succeed. Education is increasingly important to the success of both individuals and nations ... furthermore, the demands on teachers are increasing. Not only do teachers need to be able to keep order and provide useful information to students, they also need to be increasingly effective in enabling a diverse group of students to learn ever more complex material and to develop a wider range of skills. Whereas in previous decades teachers were expected to prepare only a small minority for the most ambitious intellectual work, they are now expected to prepare virtually all students for higher-order thinking and performance skills once reserved for only a few. (p. 2)

So how do we support teachers as they grapple with the expectations of high standards and inherent challenges presented in the complexity of the classroom? In concert with the voices of so many who have come before me, I suggest that it makes sense to apply findings from the neuro- and cognitive sciences to instill, foster, and support teachers' professional growth. Teachers enter the profession with beliefs, knowledge, and experiences that affect what and how they learn, and these existing constructs must be attended to. They construct knowledge and develop expertise through experiences, deliberate practice, and productive reflection in collaboration with peers. Preparing students in a knowledge economy calls for the possession of deep content knowledge by the teacher, a solid understanding about the brain and the science of learning, an understanding of how to leverage this knowledge in the classroom, and a renewed vision of what it is that students need to know and be able to do. Getting teachers to this level of expertise calls for a community of practice *of* teachers, *for* teachers, and *by* teachers with earnest support from administrators and other stakeholders. In this community of practice, teachers should be empowered as learners and co-constructors of knowledge as they work with peers and leaders in their schools to determine learning goals and best practices for attaining them.

Preparing students for success in a knowledge economy. The role of education, and therefore of classroom teachers, is to prepare students to lead productive lives as they grow and develop throughout childhood; to prepare them for life after high school; and for success in college, the workforce, and in their personal lives. Technological advances and the rapid pace that society, business, and industry changes call for a distinctive set of knowledge and skills in order to work productively within them. Teaching at this level requires expert knowledge by teachers and a shift in what has traditionally been taught in the classroom and how it has been taught, and thus a revised plan for preparing teachers to meet the challenge.

It is well known that business and industry have long lamented our graduates' lack of preparation for success in the workforce, and as a result, call for K-12 education to provide deeper learning experiences and the development of twenty-first-century skills. Additionally, colleges and universities contend with matriculating students who are underprepared. These students often have surface knowledge (due in part to the response to high-stakes testing) but are ill equipped to think critically about the content or regulate their own learning.

To address the problem and work toward deeper learning, three interconnected constructs should become part of the learning landscape: formative assessment, an incremental theory of intelligence (growth mindset), and metacognition. A vehicle metaphor can be used to conceptualize the interrelatedness of formative assessment, growth mindset, and metacognition. In this metaphor, formative assessment represents the vehicle that carries students toward their goals of deep learning and personal agency. Yet the vehicle must be driven on and by wheels of growth mindset and metacognitive skills—necessary components that both support and guide the process. Students will monitor their own growth and adjust their learning strategies through the processes of *formative assessment* more readily if (1) they have a belief that it will do some good, that their intelligence can be grown—in other words if they hold an *incremental theory of intelligence*, and (2) if they have the *metacognitive skills* necessary to do so. It does not do much good for students to have an incremental theory of intelligence if they are not provided the opportunities or lack the regulatory skills to act on those beliefs. The very process of formative assessment's Where Am I Going? Where Am I Now? and How Can I Close the Gap? provides concrete opportunities to do so. Keep in mind, however, that these constructs must be enacted in a constructivist learning environment if they are to proffer returns including deep, effective learning.

Deep learning is characterized by the ability of students to (1) discern critical concepts from less important ones, (2) relate new ideas and concepts to previous knowledge and experience, (3) put knowledge into a conceptual framework, looking for and identifying patterns, (4) retrieve and apply information appropriately, (5) evaluate new ideas and relate them to conclusions, (6) understand dialogue through which knowledge is created, (7) examine the logic of an argument critically, and (8) reflect on their own understanding and their own process of learning (Chew, 2014; Sawyer, 2014). Ultimately, understanding is developed and demonstrated when a student takes what was learned in one situation and applies it to a new situation, or when *transfer* occurs.

> Through deeper learning (which often involves shared learning and interactions with others in a community), the individual develops expertise in a particular domain of knowledge and/or performance. The product of deeper learning is transferable knowledge, including content knowledge in a domain and knowledge of how, why, and when to apply this knowledge to answer questions and solve problems. (National Research Council, 2013, pp. Sum-4)

Effective Professional Development

Numerous research studies over the past few decades have focused on teacher learning and how it takes place, and a consensus has emerged about evidence-based, distinguishing features of effective professional development (Darling-Hammond, Hyler, & Gardner, 2017). According to Darling-Hammond, et al., (p. v-vi) effective professional development:

Is content focused: Instructional strategies that teachers learn are contextual and discipline specific.
Incorporates active learning: Teachers are actively engaged as learners, not passive recipients of information. They participate in activities that serve two purposes—they construct new knowledge about learners and learning while designing and trying out teaching strategies for their students.
Supports collaboration: Teachers co-construct knowledge as they share ideas and reflect on the success of their efforts within their own communities of practice.
Uses models of effective practice: Effective models are used as a framework for PD so that teachers are able experience the model as learners, and so that they can develop of vision of what best practices look like.
Provides coaching and expert support: Teachers receive coaching and support based on their individual needs.
Offers feedback and reflection: Teachers have built-in time to reflect on the success of their efforts and to seek and receive feedback.
Is of sustained duration: Effective PD allows teachers time for practice-centered inquiry as they try out new strategies, reflect on learning outcomes, determine if the strategies were effective or not, and if not, adjust their instructional practices once again in an ongoing effort to improve.

This sets a high bar and is difficult to implement at-scale, which is crucial if we are ever going to significantly move the needle toward large-scale reform. Traditional INSET professional development is clearly not structured to meet these criteria. However, other programs have demonstrated great success implementing effective PD practices and thus effecting change (see Darling-Hammond et al., 2017 for a summary of effective PD programs), but they are often limited to a select subset of in-service teachers—generally those who participate in grant-funded initiatives or university partnerships. One possibility for broader impact lies within PLCs that have the ability to incorporate several of these effective elements into their existing structures, providing on-the-job, contextual learning. "This collaborative and job-embedded PD can be a source of efficacy and confidence for teachers, and can result in widespread improvement within and beyond the school level" (Darling-Hammond et al., 2017, p. vi).

Professional Learning Communities. PLCs take many forms, but for our purposes, they are defined as small groups of teachers with similar teaching assignments and shared teaching and learning goals that meet regularly throughout the year to focus on issues related to student learning. PLCs emerged during the mid-1990s and are now commonplace within many US schools, making them an ideal platform for professional growth for a large number of in-service teachers. However, PLCs in their current state are often loosely conceived and tend to vary considerably in design, constituency, leadership, purpose, and practice, and their effectiveness in building teacher capacity is too often capricious. Developing teacher capacity—the dispositions, knowledge, skills, and abilities that help students succeed—is a purported intermediary aim of PLCs with enhanced student achievement being the ultimate goal; however, many PLCs fall short. Many PLCs lack leadership and direction and often default to business as usual—taking care of managerial or other tasks during their designated time—rather than engaging in high-quality teacher learning.

The organization and management of PLCs have presented a challenge to school leaders since their inception. Often, PLCs are teacher-led and function without skilled teacher-leaders (TLs), thus reducing their potential to promote growth and build capacity. Functional PLCs call for effective leadership and focused design, purpose, and implementation all coupled with a degree of accountability. The campus principal plays an important role in creating and maintaining a safe environment, sharing the responsibility for change with the members of the PLC, and nurturing the teachers as they grow. However, logistics normally preclude the principal from attending or leading PLC meetings; therefore, leadership skills in teachers must be nurtured and developed if they are to be successful, and if we are going to apply the model to scale and expect positive results.

An example of a powerful and effective PLC is depicted in a study of science teachers conducted by Richmond and Manokore (2011) in which teacher learning and growth was substantial; however, leadership remained an issue. In this study, teacher discourse was examined during PLC meetings of an urban-based group of elementary science teachers as part of a 5-year project designed to foster reform-based teaching. The aim of the project was to establish and maintain grade-specific PLCs that would then serve as the backbone for improving the effectiveness of teaching. The researchers, who also served as project leaders, aspired to help the participants develop disciplinary knowledge, understand students' ideas and how they learned science, implement standards- and research-based methods for teaching science, and recognize, critique, and adapt exemplary science curricula.

Professional Development Cycle. The participants of the project were elementary teachers from different campuses within a large district who had a desire to improve their science instruction. Their participation in the PD was voluntary. The teachers initially attended a 7- to 10-day Summer Learning Institute (SLI) designed to set the stage for sustained professional development that would occur within PLCs during the academic year. At the beginning of the SLI, teachers were asked about their motivations for joining the project along with questions about their perceived strengths and learning goals. During the SLI, teachers strengthened their content knowledge and worked together to discover student concepts and misconceptions about the content in preparation for reviewing related curriculum, activities, and assessments. This information was used to construct goals for the coming school year PLC meetings. The teachers met biweekly during the school year and implemented, reflected on, and refined the selected units of study according to the agenda set during the SLI. The researchers provided additional teaching resources (videotapes, co-teaching, and debriefing activities) to enhance and expand appropriate learning opportunities. In addition, they facilitated the teachers' ongoing analysis of student work and the efficacy of implemented teaching strategies. The process was cyclical and progressive; therefore, at the end of the year, the group identified the next focus unit to be investigated and refined for the following year.

During the biweekly PLC meetings, teachers discussed their progress, shared teaching materials, reviewed their curriculum to assure it aligned with the learning targets, and reviewed formative and summative assessment items. They discussed the level and nature of student engagement, misconceptions, and challenges with implementing the curriculum and the needs and manner to improve it. Under the guidance of an expert, this PLC provided "a structured opportunity, guided by common goals, and accepted norms for participation and learning, which enabled teachers to share their teaching experiences with their PLC colleagues, thereby creating the foundation for positive changes in the quantity and quality of attention to curriculum, assessment and eventually, classroom practice" (p. 559).

Analysis of teacher discourse revealed several important elements that emerged as a result of the ongoing PLC/PD. First, the collaborative act of sharing resources, both physical and intellectual, resulted in learning by the participants who grew in both content and pedagogical content knowledge. Second, a professional community with a shared vision emerged as participants were interdependent, leveraging one another's expertise and experiences in pursuit of enabling students to learn science in meaningful ways. The participants reported that they grew to rely upon each other even outside of the scheduled PLCs, frequently communicating by phone or email, indicators of a strong community of learners. Third, the participants grew in their confidence to teach science as both their content and pedagogical content knowledge grew. Furthermore, their increased confidence created an atmosphere where they felt comfortable sharing instructional practices with colleagues more readily. Fourth, their interdependence and interaction resulted in a layer of accountability to one another that increased their dedication to improvement and success as they regularly reported back to their peers. Conversely, accountability measures of their district diverted attention from science instruction to areas that were more heavily tested—in this case, mathematics and language arts. While most of their school colleagues succumbed to the pressure of prioritizing mathematics and language arts to the neglect of science instruction, the project participants reported that despite these constraints, they felt compelled, prepared, and willing to maintain science instruction as a priority, revealing a level of strategic knowledge that others in their school did not exhibit.

Sustainability was a fifth element that emerged, and it warrants discussion. As previously identified, several factors have the potential to jeopardize PLC sustainability as well as the scaling-up of this type of reform effort. The most significant factor is the dependence upon external facilitation. In this project, the external facilitator kept the participants on track and provided a layer of expertise that was relied upon throughout the year. Clearly, in most US schools, PLCs operate without this advantage, and the potential for success of any community of practice is diminished without the guidance of a dedicated and capable leader.

Some entities have addressed this issue by creating resource materials that have the potential to prepare and empower teachers as facilitators and provide guidance and resources to lead them through the process. *Classroom*

Assessment for Student Learning: Doing It Right-Using It Well (CASL) (Chappuis, 2009) is an example of a credible resource that teachers can use for assistance in promoting a community of teacher learners without the help of an outside expert. This and other such resource materials provide reliable information and pathways for attainable solutions for school districts that do not have access to an expert facilitator.

For PLCs not using this type of resource, and even for those that do, a leader is still needed to guide the teachers through the process in order to facilitate optimum teacher learning and growth. The most readily available human resources for leadership are the in-service teachers that work on the campus and are intimately familiar with the culture and conditions therein. Teacher-Leader Models (TLM) are emerging that empower teachers to become leaders in their own districts (Riveros, Newton, & da Costa, 2013), and these models have great potential to effect change if implemented strategically. However, TLs need targeted and appropriate professional development themselves in order to effectively lead PLCs and carry out the mission and achieve the goals of the district. Hence, the idea of cascading professional development wherein the "expert" (perhaps the school district's Curriculum and Instruction specialist or a consultant) works with TLs (usually department heads or other designated district PLC leaders) who provide leadership to their colleagues at the campus level. Guiding the TLs requires quality professional development as described earlier in that it should be content focused, active, and collaborative, providing models of effective practice and ongoing coaching and support. Additionally, TLs will need leadership and facilitation development to prepare them for their new role. A combination of focused training (like the SLI model) for the TLs led by an expert and then sustained through ongoing TL PLCs provides opportunities for significant growth that can then be shared with teachers at the campus-level PLCs.

Desired PLC outcomes. The aim of PLCs is to provide a platform for teachers to learn from their own experiences and from each other as they refine their craft and build capacity, all with the goal of improving student outcomes. Central to this aim is PCI—a system of inquiry wherein teachers critique their own pedagogy through scaffolded critical reflection on their own and other teachers' practice (Long, 2012, p. 145). PCI has long been a vehicle for teacher professional growth and the impetus for conceptual change. As teachers are exposed to new concepts or strategies, they transfer what they have learned to their own classroom and reflect on its success. Did it accomplish the learning goal(s) set forth? If not, why not? Was it appropriately aligned with the learning goals? What went well? What did not? What could be done differently to improve? Questions such as this pepper the reflection process. Self-monitoring—the ability to attend to our actions, curiosity to examine the effects of those actions, and willingness to use those observations to improve behavior and patterns of thinking (Epstein, Siegel, & Silberman, 2008)—has been shown to alter attention and attention regulating neural pathways. As teachers practice and reflect, they construct new knowledge or refine existing knowledge, experiencing conceptual change, thus strengthening or altering their mental model of learning. (This is clearly an over-simplification of the neurocognitive processes of learning—of which there is a rich body of research that supports it—but it is provided in this manner here in the interest of brevity.)

This inquiry process should be enriched and supported by feedback from PLC colleagues, who may reframe the narrative, offering insight from a different perspective. Teachers receiving the feedback must be open and willing to consider the reasoning and perspectives of others. The exchange should occur in an accepting and stress-free atmosphere as stress and anxiety are known to limit the ability to analyze and synthesize information (Paul, Elder, & Bartell, 1997), and cognitive behaviors that are important to the process of growth. The process of feedback and reflection leads to a re-assessment of the purpose of the activity, and the planning and implementation of future activities (see the ADM, Fig. 4.2 as reminder). This recursive, inquiry process of implement-reflect-adjust restructures the brain (Ludvik, 2016) as it constructs knowledge about the nature of learners and learning. PCI has the potential to debunk faulty knowledge and beliefs about learners and learning while replacing them with a more accurate representation, which is critical to learner-centered instruction and student success.

The bigger picture and systems thinking. Not only do teachers need to self-monitor as they consider the effects of their teaching behaviors, they also need to think systemically and recognize the interconnectedness of various aspects of teaching that arises over time. Thus, teachers should adopt a systems approach to understanding the complexity of teaching and learning. A system, according to Peter Senge, et al. in his book *The Dance of Change* (1999), "is anything that takes its integrity and form from the ongoing interaction of its parts ... Systems are defined by the fact that their elements have a common purpose and behave in common ways, precisely because they are interrelated toward that purpose" (p. 137). Systems thinking is an approach to understanding that examines the linkages and interactions of the constituent parts of the entire system. As we know, teaching is not linear, rather it is a complex ecosystem with dynamic, interdependent, overlapping, and interlocking elements, and the success of the whole depends on its parts. Altering a part changes the whole to some extent, whether great or small, and those correlations and consequences should be examined if we are to have a deeper understanding of the nature of learning.

There are a number of tools that help make sense of the interrelated parts within a system such as feedback loops (Furtak, 2016), program logic models (He, Rohr, Miller, Levin, & Mercier, 2010; Yin, 2009), and concept or causal maps. Another tool, a behavior over time (BOT) graph, also has the potential to build capacity as teachers work to understand the system and collaborate with their peers to enhance practice (Calancie, Anderson, Branscomb, Apostolico, & Lich, 2018).

> ...drawing BOT graphs, annotating the events and systemic forces that are likely to influence the depicted trends, and then discussing the graphs in a diverse group provides an opportunity ... to hear each other's perspectives and creates a more holistic understanding of the key factors that contribute to a trend. (p. 1)

Although the Calancie study investigated the use of BOT graphs in the public health arena, the analytic tool readily adapts to the complex world of education as well. To design a BOT graph, the behaviors of interest (the dependent variables) are plotted along the vertical y axis, and time (the independent variable) runs along the horizontal x axis. The behaviors can be anything that changes over time. For example, it could be the amount of group work that students participate in during class or the amount of time that the teacher spends lecturing, and so on. To determine variables that should be graphed, the PLC participants discuss behaviors that they observe changing, or ones they think *should* change, in light of the goals set by the PLC and the learning that is taking place. Then, once the graphs have been generated, analysis would occur through the group discussion of questions such as:

- What changes do we note?
- What caused any changes in direction or slope?
- What changes may happen in the future based on what has been happening?
- Do we see any connections (interdependencies or causal relationships) between or among the lines? What do they mean? How are they related?

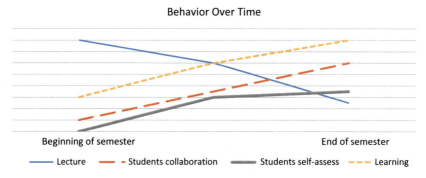

Fig. 6.1 Hypothetical behavior over time graph

The group analysis of the BOT graph leads to deep rich discussions that have the potential to change mental models of learning and improve practice as teachers discover for themselves the consequences of their teaching behaviors. See Fig. 6.1 for a sample BOT graph for educators involved in a PLC that focuses on formative assessment.

PORTRAIT OF A TWENTY-FIRST-CENTURY TEACHER

Regardless of the approach to or purpose of professional development initiatives that are put in place, the demands of teaching compel us to develop teachers who understand how students learn, and subsequently:

- Are equipped and willing to design and implement constructivist learning environments,
- See themselves as designer, architect, and facilitator of learning,
- Are equipped and willing to empower students, and
- Are adaptive and reflective—life-long learners themselves.

Developing teachers with these essential qualities lays a healthy foundation of rich, fertile soil that can be cultivated for more targeted growth within specific content areas once established. These qualities are foundational to future growth, and without them, we may be sowing seeds in shallow, rocky, or sandy soil, hindering productivity and limiting the effects of our efforts.

Professional Development: What's Missing?

As we prepare teachers to flourish in the twenty-first-century, developing an expertise in formative assessment should be a top priority. There are a host of resources that school districts and PLCs can use to guide the process of learning how to effectively implement formative assessment strategies into existing curriculum. Additionally, we must address the underlying constructs that have the potential to deepen the knowledge base of teachers and strengthen their content knowledge needed about the science of learning to provide more meaningful and applicable learning experiences for students. The following narrative provides professional development design elements that will strengthen the teacher's learning experience, and suggestions for fundamental conceptual understandings that should be developed in teachers and students as well. The additional design elements and enriched content have the potential to elevate teacher and student learning to a new level, transforming the classroom in order to meet the needs of twenty-first-century learners.

The foundational design elements of effective PLCs include utilization of the following: (1) backward design to establish a framework for learning and growth, (2) the processes of formative assessment to move the learning forward and empower teacher participants, and (3) the study of the learning sciences including targeted instruction intended to give teachers the necessary skills to promote both a growth mindset and metacognitive acuity in their students.

Backward design. In Chap. 2, we discussed using Wiggins and McTighe's backward design to plan learning activities for the classroom. Likewise, backward design provides a useful framework for planning professional development initiatives as well—a design element that is often neglected. As per Wiggins and McTighe's well-known mantra, successful planning begins with the end in mind. Stage 1 calls for an identification of the desired results of the program. What are the big ideas that teachers should grasp and own? For example, an overarching theme for the study of formative assessment might include the idea that formative assessment has the potential to equip and empower students to become self-regulated learners as they think critically about the content and about their own cognition. Subsequent overarching goals, essential questions, and learning targets are set along with specific understandings that are important for the teachers to acquire. For example, essential questions might include "What is formative assessment?," "What are the benefits of using the processes of formative assessment?," and "How can I implement these practices into existing curriculum?" Articulating the knowledge and skills related to effective implementation of formative assessment would follow, maintaining alignment with the overarching goals and big ideas. Stage 2 calls for a determination of acceptable evidence to indicate growth or mastery of the concepts. In considering what evidence could be used by teachers to demonstrate mastery of formative assessment, a wide range of evaluation tools might include (1) growth portfolios with artifacts such as student work followed by a reflective narrative, (2) observations by colleagues or others, (3) teacher evaluations, (4) video documentation, or (5) lesson plan revisions. The next stage, Stage 3, requires the planning of learning experiences. As agendas are formulated for each PLC, it is critical that they consist of learner-centered, active, sustained, collaborative, and reflective activities that both align with the established goals and provide evidence of mastery or growth. Equally important is the realization that these processes should be a collaborative effort. Teachers must have input into the development of goals as well as in determining what represents evidence of mastery.

When constructing both the learning experiences and the PLCs, Dylan Wiliam, in *Leadership for Teacher Learning* (2016), suggested a "signature pedagogy" to be applied specifically to teacher learning in regards to formative assessment. Wiliam suggested the following 6 activities for each meeting: (1) an introduction where learning targets for the meeting are clarified, (2) a starter activity that turns participants' minds to the meeting, (3) a time for feedback where participants share their formative assessment experiences and others offer constructive suggestions, (4) new learning to increase knowledge, perhaps through readings, videos, or other media, (5) personal action planning or goal setting, and (6) a brief wrap up.

Developing a backward design plan for professional development is time consuming and rarely straightforward, but it is well worth the investment of time and energy. The very process of collaborative planning forges a shared vision for the group, and the finished product serves as a useful framework and point of reference throughout. It makes the learning targets clear and empowers teachers in their own professional growth as they plan the learning experiences. Additionally, backward design planning ensures that the initiative focuses on the intended outcomes and that the planned activities and assessments align with the program goals.

A meta-use of formative assessment. The second component that is often missing from professional development is the inclusion of formative assessment. The process of formative assessment during teacher professional development is essential for teacher learning, just like it is for students. Chapter 2 discussed practical ways to empower students through FA, collaboration, feedback, self- and peer assessment, goal setting, and monitoring one's own progress. These same principles apply to teacher learning. To be explicit, let's apply the three overarching goals of formative assessment that center around these questions of "Where Am I Going?," "Where Am I Now?," and "How Can I Close the Gap?" to teacher professional development. Underlying this process is an assumption that the environment for teacher learning is risk-tolerant and emotionally safe, where teachers serve as resources for one another in pursuit of fulfilling a shared vision. Moreover, they strengthen their strategic knowledge through PCI, thus exemplifying the attributes of a life-long learner. Teachers ultimately own the learning and take responsibility for themselves and each other, thinking critically about content, pedagogy, and student outcomes.

Where Am I Going? The desired outcomes of the professional development initiative, including goals, learning targets, success criteria, and evidence of mastery or growth, should be established early on through backward design. The desired outcomes should not be a directive from above but rather be co-constructed by all participants of the PLC taking into consideration teachers' prior knowledge, experiences, and beliefs about learners and learning. Attributes of quality teaching should be clarified, modeled, examined, and analyzed, debunking misconceptions about teaching and learning with a continued focus on learning goals rather than on performance. In other words, a constant consideration of questions such as "Does this strategy result in learning?," "How do we know?," and "What evidence is there to support it?"

A convenient way to examine a wide range of teaching practices is through the use of video analysis. Video analysis offers an opportunity to examine good teaching practices that are rarely observed in the traditional classroom (Seidel, Stürmer, Blomberg, Kobarg, & Schwindt, 2011). Additionally, teachers frequently ask to see other teachers' classrooms in action, considering the process a powerful way to understand how ideas can translate into practice, but their schedules often conflict, making videos a viable alternative (Fishman, Davis, & Chan, 2014, p. 715). Care should be taken in selection of materials to analyze, but when chosen appropriately, video-clips of teachers and students in situ have great potential for productive analysis, leading to clarity about aspects of quality teaching and learning. For example, in my experience working with pre-service and in-service teachers alike, I have found they often have difficulty imagining secondary math instruction that is constructivist and learner-centered, having been exposed primarily to traditional, didactic math instruction as students. To provide a model of constructivist instruction in math, participants watch a video that is produced by the Annenberg Foundation Professional Development Series entitled *Insights into Algebra I: Teaching for Learning—Workshop 4—Quadratic Functions*. This 58-minute video showcases learner-centered instruction that follows a 5E Learning Cycle model. The participants take guided notes during viewing that focuses on the sequence of the lesson, the role of the teacher, the role of the student, assessment practices throughout, and the level of thinking that takes place using Bloom's taxonomy as a guide. They watch the video on their own or with their peers prior to coming to class and then use class time to engage in deep analysis and rich discussion of the practices observed. This activity is one way to answer "Where Am I Going?," providing a model of learner-centered instruction that may be new to them. Other video resources made publicly available through educational entities also provide a variety of examples that can be used for analysis of teaching practices.

Where Am I Now? The metacognitive practice of reflection and self-assessment has been shown to increase the degree that a person transfers their learning to new settings and events (Bransford et al., 2000, p. 12). Transferability—the ability to use knowledge appropriately and fruitfully in a new or different context from that in which it was initially learned (Wiggins & McTighe, 2005)—followed by productive reflection fosters conceptual change and consequently new theories about teaching and learning. As teachers work together in their PLCs, they must continually monitor where they are on the learning bridge. This can be done with help and feedback from their PLC colleagues as well as through self-assessment and goal setting.

Feedback is by far one of the most important tools for advancing learning. Often referred to as success-intervention feedback, it involves recognizing what went well, pointing out things that did not go well, then providing direction or suggestions for improvement. It is important to differentiate between feedback and a critique. As an illustration, consider the difference between the following scenarios shared in a recent conversation with two of my colleagues. Both had a problem with using a confident voice in front of students. One colleague received this "feedback" from her administrator: "I don't know why your voice was so shaky and high-pitched during the lesson; you sounded scared (shaking his head with bewilderment)." Contrast that with the feedback another colleague received: "Ms. Jones, the instructions you gave were important, and you said all the right things; however, the students couldn't really hear what you were saying. Try lowering your voice and projecting with confidence. If you want to hear someone who does a good job at this, go next door, and listen to Ms. Ramirez. She's got it down." There is a big difference here. The former is simply criticism with no suggestions for improvement, and the latter is helpful and has the potential to promote growth. The same can be said for written feedback. Feedback that only points out problems without providing something positive coupled with suggestions for improvement is unproductive. It lacks the potential to help teachers grow and is likely to discourage them from trying. And without feedback, the likelihood of recognizing mistakes or misguided ideas is greatly diminished.

A powerful tool for self-assessment occurs through video analysis of teachers' classroom practice through individual and group reflection. Congruent with the consensus model of professional development, using video analysis grounds teachers' analyses in context (Taylor, Roth, Wilson, Stuhlsatz, & Tipton, 2017) and allows them to look closely at teaching and learning. Video analysis should be guided by a set of reflective questions that concentrate the attention on learning. The protocol used by Taylor et al. (2017, p. 16) as part of their Science Teachers Learning through Lesson Analysis (STeLLA) professional development serves as a good example. STeLLA relied on a lesson analysis protocol to keep the discussion on track. Teachers analyzed video from each other's classrooms and discussed the use of particular strategies, responding individually to targeted questions about the learning taking place by writing down a claim, evidence, reasoning, and an alternative. Teachers shared their observations with each other as the teacher featured in the video listened, and the featured teacher then discussed with the group what she learned both from listening to her peers and from her own observations, building individual capacity and a shared vision of quality instruction, what Fishman et al. (2014, p. 715) called a *professional vision*—the ability to see and interpret critical features of classroom events.

Roth et al. (2017) conducted research on STeLLA's impact on upper elementary teacher and student learning and found that teachers who participated in the study (1) developed deep content knowledge, (2) developed stronger abilities to use pedagogical content knowledge, and (3) increased their use of effective teaching strategies. And most importantly, their students' learning improved significantly (p. 4).

And finally, goal setting also acts as a powerful metacognitive action that teachers can employ as they determine what their learning gaps are and how to bridge them. In a meta-analysis of the power of a case-based approach to learning, Kolodner (2006) contended that "learning will happen best in contexts of trying to achieve goals of interest" (p. 227). Years of research have validated the importance of goal setting, revealing that it has the potential to lead to higher performance, particularly when the goals are specific and challenging, and based on an accurate analysis of the gap that exists. Likewise, as mental models shift and re-form through the learning experience, goals should evolve accordingly.

How Can I Close the Gap? In building teacher capacity, as teachers work toward gaining the strategic knowledge and related skills needed to bridge the gap toward mastery of teaching, the process must be made visible to them, and evidence generated from the process should be used to make decisions about what's next. Developing expertise calls for knowing what specific behaviors need to be refined. This insight is followed by deliberate practice, feedback, and skilled coaching within the PLC. "Both the feedback and the collegial nature of the process appear to stimulate reflection and greater skill development" (Hammerness, Darling-Hammond, & Bransford, 2005). The concept of deliberate practice was introduced in the early 1990s by Ericsson, Krampe, and Tesch-Romer (1993) but gained prominence in the literature through publications by psychologist Angela Lee Duckworth. Duckworth et al. (2011) claimed that the way to improve and develop expertise is through deliberate practice that

> entails engaging in a focused, typically planned training activity designed to improve some aspect of performance. During deliberate practice, individuals receive immediate informative feedback on their performance and can then repeat the same or similar tasks with full attention toward changing inferior or incorrect responses, thus improving the identified area of weakness. (p. 174)

Practice alone does not improve performance or close gaps; it must be an iterative process that is deliberate, paying close attention to specific aspects that need improving, setting a goal for improvement, conducting additional practice in pursuit of the goal, followed by more reflection on its success.

The science of learning. I contend that the third component missing from professional development is the purposeful training of teachers in the science of learning. Although the neuroscience of learning is in its infancy, all teachers should have a basic understanding of the brain and how it works to construct knowledge. As the director for a science education grant program many years ago, I attended a Brain Expo in San Diego, CA—a national conference that was designed to connect what is known about the brain and learning, to practice, featuring expert researchers, speakers, and guests such as Eric Jensen—a brain-based learning expert. I was dismayed as I realized that most of the attendees were researchers and educators in higher education, not classroom teachers who needed the information the most. If we expect teachers to use the science of brain-based learning, knowledge of it must be made more readily available. Understanding the brain and how it functions provides a foundation for PCIs as teachers discover what works and what does not. Additionally, knowledge of the brain and learning sciences facilitates informed curricular decisions—helping teachers recognize and design learner-centered instruction. Ludvik, in her book *The Neuroscience of Learning and Development* (2016, p. 7), described eight such classroom pedagogies that are consistent with what we know about how students construct knowledge. They include (1) inquiry-based learning, (2) problem-based learning, (3) service learning, (4) team-based learning, (5) flipped classroom learning, (6) experiential learning, (7) self-regulated learning, and (8) contemplative learning. These constructivist pedagogies are structured in a way that has the potential to support formative assessment and lead to deep learning. The brain-based science that undergirds the pedagogies as well as practical strategies for implementation should be central to the professional development of teachers.

Furthermore, the power that stems from understanding the brain and the science of learning is reflected in the research on implicit theories of intelligence and how understanding the incremental theory of intelligence (growth mindset) impacts students and their learning. Blackwell, Trzesniewski, and Dweck (2007) studied low-achieving middle school math students, who were involved (as the experimental group) in a series of eight short seminars that focused on the physiology of the brain, study skills, and anti-stereotypic thinking. Lessons were taught that emphasized that intelligence is malleable and can be developed. The control group received the same eight seminars with identical study skills and brain development information but no information about the malleability of intelligence. There was a statistically significant difference between the achievement of the experimental and control group—providing evidence of the power of explicitly teaching students' growth mindset principles. It is reasonable to conclude that the same principle applies to adults as well.

Developing a growth mindset in teachers is essential to effective teaching. Rheinberg (as cited in Dweck, 2007) found that when teachers had a fixed mindset, the students who entered their class as low achievers left as low achievers at the end of the year. When teachers had a growth mindset, however, many of the students that started the year as low achievers moved up and became moderate or even high achievers (Dweck, 2010). Teachers with a growth mindset will model growth mindset approaches to teaching and learning and will provide growth mindset praise that has been shown to encourage and support, whereas fixed mindset praise has been shown to have detrimental effects on the learner and the learning process.

Subsequently, the learning environment within a classroom tends to be shaped by and reflects the teacher's mindset. Overall, there is evidence that a teacher's approach to challenging and encouraging students can either weaken or strengthen the ability of students to cope successfully with difficulties they will inevitably face and has significant implications for learning. Teacher training should purposefully address theories of intelligence and how they apply to instructional strategies and classroom learning behaviors. Equal attention should be paid to developing a growth mindset in teachers as well—which may emerge as they prepare to teach the concept to students, the effect of bidirectional learning. We learn by the very practice of preparing to teach.

As teachers study the science of learning and form (or re-form) their mental model of how students learn, it affects what and how they teach, shifting their role from one that transmits knowledge (if they were an instructivist teacher) to the role of designer, architect, and facilitator of learning. Such teachers plan and implement activities that support learning on a continuous basis. They work with students to learn desired patterns and levels of involvement and learning, while controlling their tendencies to revert to past thinking and practice (both for the teacher and the students). This enlightened understanding of their role as a teacher unburdens them in one respect—for those who believed it was their responsibility to produce high achievers—yet it creates an elevated bar in another as they share control with the students when the stakes are so high.

Instilling growth mindsets and developing metacognition skills. Professional development should prepare teachers to be explicit and purposeful in teaching students to have a growth mindset. It should also prepare teachers to instill, foster, and support the metacognitive skills that students need to develop an enduring growth mindset. Accordingly, growth mindset and metacognition are both a requirement *and* an outcome of the effective use of formative assessment.

These suggestions for the development of student's mindsets and regulation of cognition are predicated on the assumption that classroom practice includes effective feedback and assignment structures that support ongoing, incremental, adaptive learning opportunities. Pedagogy that supports growth mindset and metacognition cannot simply pay lip service to the idea of empowering students, rather students must have actual opportunities to take control—all under the guidance of a skilled classroom teacher.

Conclusion

This chapter expanded our vision of professional development for teachers, providing design elements and underlying constructs that should be addressed if we want to cultivate expert teachers who are equipped to prepare students in and for a new economy. Traditional systems of teacher learning have been inadequate, neglecting the important role that formative assessment plays in empowering students to be the master of their own learning and failing to recognize the underlying principles of the science of learning that are foundational to designing learner-centered environments. The goals proposed here are ambitious yet could be implemented into existing PLCs and classrooms given the right leadership. Leaders must have the strategic knowledge necessary to build a new system of learning, despite externally imposed elements that pressure them to succumb to tradition. In the following chapter, we will look at larger, systemic changes that must take place in order to alleviate the tension between what students need for twenty-first-century living and the system limitations that make it difficult to get them there.

Works Cited

Blackwell, L. S., Trzesniewski, K. H., & Dweck, C. S. (2007). Implicit theories of intelligence predict achievement across an adolescent transition: A longitudinal study and an intervention. *Child Development, 78*(1), 246–263.

Box, M. C. (2008). *Formative assessment: Patterns, personal practice assessment theories, and impact on student achievement and motivation in science* (PhD Dissertation), Texas Tech University, Lubbock, TX.

Bransford, J. D., Brown, A. L., & Cocking, R. R. (Eds.). (2000). *How people learn: Brain, mind, experience, and school*. Washington, DC: The National Academies Press.

Calancie, L., Anderson, S., Branscomb, J., Apostolico, A. A., & Lich, K. H. (2018). Using behavior over time graphs to spur systems thinking among public health practitioners. *Preventing Chronic Disease, 15*, 1–8.

Chappuis, J. (2009). *Learning team facilitator handbook: A resource for collaborative study of classroom assessment for student learning.* Educational Testing Service.

Chew, S. L. (2014). Helping students to get the most out of studying. In *Applying science of learning in education: Infusing psychological science into the curriculum* (pp. 215–225).

Darling-Hammond, L., & Bransford, J. (2005). *Preparing teachers for a changing world: What teachers should learn and be able to do.* San Francisco, CA: Jossey-Bass.

Darling-Hammond, L., Hyler, M. E., & Gardner, M. (2017). *Effective teacher professional development.* Palo Alto, CA: Learning Policy Institute.

Davis, E. A., Palincsar, A. S., Smith, P. S., Arias, A. M., & Kademian, S. M. (2017). Educative curriculum materials: Uptake, impact, and implications for research and design. *Educational Researcher, 46*(6), 293–304.

Duckworth, A. L., Kirby, T. A., Tsukayama, E., Berstein, H., & Ericsson, K. A. (2011). Deliberate practice spells success: Why grittier competitors triumph at the National Spelling Bee. *Social Psychological and Personality Science, 2*(2), 174–181.

Dweck, C. S. (2007). The perils and promises of praise. *ASCD, 65*(2), 34–39.

Dweck, C. S. (2010). Mind-sets and equitable education. *Principal Leadership, 10*(5), 26–29.

Epstein, R. M., Siegel, D. J., & Silberman, J. (2008). Self-monitoring in clinical practice: A challenge for medical educators. *Journal of Continuing Education in the Health Professions, 28*(1), 5–13.

Ericsson, K. A., Krampe, R. T., & Tesch-Römer, C. (1993). The role of deliberate practice in the acquisition of expert performance. *Psychological Review, 100*(3), 363–406.

Fishman, B. J., Davis, E. A., & Chan, C. K. (2014). A learning sciences perspective on teacher learning research. In *The Cambridge handbook of the learning sciences* (pp. 707–725). Cambridge University Press.

Furtak, E. M. (2016). *The feedback loop: Using formative assessment data for science teaching and learning.* NSTA Press.

Hammerness, K., Darling-Hammond, L., & Bransford, J. D. (2005). How teachers learn and develop. In L. Darling-Hammond & J. D. Bransford (Eds.), *Preparing teachers for a changing world: What teachers should learn and be able to do* (pp. 358–389). San Francisco, CA: Sponsored by the National Academy of Education, Jossey-Bass.

He, Y., Rohr, J., Miller, S. D., Levin, B. B., & Mercier, S. (2010). Toward continuous program improvement: Using a logic model for professional development school program evaluation. *School-University Partnerships, 4*(1), 15–28.

Kolodner, J. L. (2006). Case-based reasoning. In R. K. Sawyer (Ed.), *The Cambridge handbook of the learning sciences* (pp. 225–242). New York: Cambridge University Press.

Long, J. (2012). Changing teachers' practice through critical reflection on pedagogy. *International Journal of Interdisciplinary Social Sciences, 6*(4), 145–159.

Loucks-Horsley, S., Love, N., Stiles, K., Mundry, S., & Hewson, P. (2003). *Designing professional development for teachers of science and mathematics* (2nd ed.). Thousand Oaks, CA: Corwin Press, Inc.

Ludvik, M. J. B. (Ed.). (2016). *The neuroscience of learning and development: Enhancing creativity, compassion, critical thinking, and peace in higher education*. Sterling, VA: Stylus Publishing, LLC.

National Research Council. (2013). *Education for life and work: Developing transferable knowledge and skills in the 21st century*. Washington, DC: The National Academies Press.

Paul, R. W., Elder, L., & Bartell, T. (1997). *California teacher preparation for instruction in critical thinking: Research findings and policy recommendations*. Sacramento, CA: California Commission on Teacher Credentialing.

Popham, J. (2008). *Transformative assessment*. Alexandria, VA: Association for Supervision and Curriculum Development.

Richmond, G., & Manokore, V. (2011). Identifying elements critical for functional and sustainable professional learning communities. *Science Education, 95*(3), 543–570.

Riveros, A., Newton, P., & da Costa, J. (2013). From teachers to teacher-leaders: A case study. *International Journal of Teacher Leadership, 4*(1), 1–15.

Roth, K., Bintz, J., Wickler, N. I. Z., Hvidsten, C., Taylor, J., Beardsley, P. M., ... Wilson, C. D. (2017). Design principles for effective video-based professional development. *International Journal of STEM Education, 4*(1), 1.

Sawyer, R. K. (Ed.). (2014). *The Cambridge handbook of the learning sciences* (2nd ed.). New York, NY: Cambridge University Press.

Seidel, T., Stürmer, K., Blomberg, G., Kobarg, M., & Schwindt, K. (2011). Teacher learning from analysis of videotaped classroom situations: Does it make a difference whether teachers observe their own teaching or that of others? *Teaching and Teacher Education, 27*(2), 259–267.

Senge, P., Kleiner, A., Roberts, C., Ross, R., Roth, G., Smith, B., & Guman, E. C. (1999). *The dance of change: The challenges to sustaining momentum in learning organizations*. New York, NY: Doubleday.

Taylor, J. A., Roth, K., Wilson, C. D., Stuhlsatz, M. A., & Tipton, E. (2017). The effect of an analysis-of-practice, videocase-based, teacher professional development program on elementary students' science achievement. *Journal of Research on Educational Effectiveness, 10*(2), 241–271.

Wiggins, G., & McTighe, J. (2005). *Understanding by design* (2nd ed.). Alexandria, VA: Association for Supervision and Curriculum Development.

Wiliam, D. (2016). *Leadership for teacher learning: Creating a culture where all teachers improve so that all students succeed.* West Palm Beach: Learning Sciences International.

Yin, R. (Ed.). (2009). *Case study research: Design and methods* (Vol. 5, 4th ed.). Thousand Oaks: Sage.

CHAPTER 7

Systemic Change

The case studies of Mary, Monica, and Phoebe presented in this monograph along with an informative body of research have revealed a level of systemic change that needs to take place if we are to transform education to include reform practices such as formative assessment. The aim of formative assessment is to equip and empower students to become self-regulated, life-long learners in an environment that deepens the learning as students think critically about the content and about their own cognition. In the case studies presented here, it was evident that Mary and Monica's mental models of learning led them to teach in a manner that did not result in deep learning, and they lacked strategic knowledge to address the discrepancies. Externally imposed elements that had significant potential to shape their PPATs in a positive manner were either absent or misdirected. For example, the teachers lacked a system of professional development that would help them grow, and they were driven by teacher and curricular standards that focused on factual knowledge rather than on core ideas and 21st century skills. And most certainly for Mary and Monica, like most other teachers in the United States, the requirements of high-stakes testing that calls for a curriculum that is a mile-wide and an inch deep affirmed teaching practices that support the game of schooling rather than satisfying the true goal of education—that of learning. In this chapter, we will examine three systemic changes that need to take place in order to make reform practices such as formative assessment part of the landscape: grading systems, teacher preparation and evaluation systems, and curricular standards and related standardized tests.

© The Author(s) 2019
C. Box, *Formative Assessment in United States Classrooms*,
https://doi.org/10.1007/978-3-030-03092-6_7

Grading Systems

In 1897, Mount Holyoke University established the following grading scale: A Excellent (95–100), B Good (85–94), C Fair (76–84), D Passed (75), E Failed (Below 75). Look familiar? It should. Many K-12 schools still cling to an A-F grading system very similar to this one that was established over 100 years ago for colleges and universities. It arose during the Progressive period in concert with the Taylorism era of standardization that dominated the educational landscape and mysteriously endures to this day. Although grade parameters have shifted slightly (90–100 = A, 80–89 = B, 70–79 = C, and below 70 is a failing grade), not much else has changed. Conventional US grading and reporting systems include the following general features:

1. A grade is given for an individual assignment (in-class or homework) that normally covers a wide variety of objectives. The assigned grade is an arbitrary number that represents many variables and is not necessarily based on a particular standard.
2. Individual grades are aggregated, weighted, and averaged to determine the final grade for the marking period (normally 6- or 9-week periods). Often, one semester exam is weighted as heavily as an entire marking period within a semester. Then, all marking period grades plus the semester exam are averaged together for a final grade that determines whether or not a student gets academic credit for the course.
3. During the marking period, all assignment grades (homework, quizzes, daily work) are recorded and averaged from the beginning to the end of the period. Zeroes are entered for missing assignments. Students are therefore penalized for missing work and low scores at the beginning of the marking period, thus the final grade does not represent their ultimate level of mastery.
4. Final grades for a marking period may be assigned from a normative perspective as teachers may curve grades based on the overall performance of the group.
5. Grades are reported as a single letter or numerical grade for each discipline, such as, algebra, history, biology, and so on.

Over time, in addition to the general features described above, the system evolved to include using grades for classroom management purposes as well, being leveraged to coax students into compliance on grounds of fostering and rewarding responsibility and moral behavior. For example, in many classrooms, points have been deducted from assignments for various reasons such as neglecting to write a name on a paper, messiness, or heading structure. Conversely, bonus points have been awarded for answering "extra credit" questions at the end of a test or assignment (that may or may not have anything to do with the content), bringing supplies, returning permission slips, participation, or any other number of school-sanctioned initiatives. During my tenure as a middle school science teacher, a principal required all teachers to give a daily grade of 100 to students who were "dressed for success" that day, just one example of how schools have used grades to manipulate behavior. Grading has also been used to regulate morality, remnants from our earliest days in history when colonists believed that the establishment of schools was for the purpose of moral education. Therefore, grades have been used as a penalty for cheating, laziness, misbehavior or inattention during an activity, or turning in late work (typically speaking: one day late—10 points, two days late—20, three days late—30, more than three days late, the student received a zero), and they have also been used to reward honesty, industry, punctuality, and the like. These penalties have been ostensibly levied to teach students to be responsible, but for many teachers, have served as leverage in order to manage the overwhelming task of keeping up with grading and organizing student work. A matter of convenience, if you will.

Put this way by Vatterott (2015), "We reward responsibility, effort, hard work, neatness, and homework completion. We penalize tardiness, sloppiness, late work, and cheating. For this noble goal of instilling morality in students, grades have been a most convenient tool. Unfortunately, this use of grades has led to a school culture that often places more value on compliance and working than learning" (p. 7). Over time, then we have fused behavioral and learning outcomes, binding them into one grade and claiming that grade as an overall indicator of student accomplishment and achievement.

This conventional grading system that blends haphazard behavior management measures with inefficient and inaccurate reports of learning has resulted in grades that do not directly correlate to the purported assessment and are used for purposes of great consequence. Not only are grades used to communicate with students and parents how well the student is doing in school, they have also been used to rank and compare students, to track them into advanced or on-level courses, to decide eligibility for extra-curricular activities, to confer course credit and determine eligibility for graduation, and for college scholarship and matriculation purposes. Indeed, GPAs both open doors and close them whether students are prepared for what is beyond them or not.

More importantly, however, conventional grading results in an indiscriminate, inaccurate reporting of what students know and can do and decidedly does very little to improve learning. Students learn to "game" the system, and many of them spend more time and energy playing the grade game than learning. This is concerning in an era of high-stakes testing and accountability where it is important to know exactly what students know and can do in tested content areas, but is especially troublesome for educators and students if it is harmful to the process of learning.

Thus, our dependence upon and fixation with grades and GPAs creates a mindset that is antithetical to the ultimate goal of education—the goal of learning. The proliferation of high-stakes testing combined with traditional instruction and instructivist practices promotes a grade-oriented mentality that is incompatible with learner-centered instruction and the processes of formative assessment. Therefore, in order to shift the emphasis from achievement, performance, and grades, we need to create an environment that focuses on learning and producing evidence of mastery toward our learning goals. See Table 7.1 for indicators of a grade vs. learning-oriented environment.

This shift to a focus on learning requires a systemic change in not only our curriculum and instruction but in our grading practices as well. Conventional grading is teacher centered, promotes and supports a fixed mindset, does not support incremental growth, and recognizes performance and achievement; not at all congruent with learner-centered instruction and the processes of formative assessment. Fortunately, there is a movement sweeping the nation as many schools have recognized the problems with conventional grading and have begun to use "standards-based grading"—an alternative approach.

Standards-based grading (SBG) is a system where grades are earned based on mastery of discreet standards, or one that "references student achievement to specific topics within each subject area" (Marzano, 2011, p. 17). SBG is a shift from norm-referenced grading that compares students to each other, to criterion-reference grading where clear criteria are communicated to students, and they are graded based on their individual progress to meet the criteria, irrespective of how their peers are doing. Teachers differentiate their instruction based on student needs, and teachers and students alike know exactly what concepts or skills students have mastered and what still needs work.

Table 7.1 A comparison of a grade vs. learning mentality

A grade-oriented mentality	A learning-oriented mentality
Purpose	
The purpose of assessment is to assign grades	The purpose of assessment is to determine mastery
The purpose of grades is to rank students	The purpose of grades is to let students know how close they are to achieving their learning goals
The purpose of report cards is to communicate to parents, to state and federal educational entities, and to colleges and universities a student's level of achievement	The purpose of report cards is to serve as an indicator of a student's readiness to function productively beyond their current position, to be shared with students, parents, state and federal educational entities, and colleges and universities
Classroom practices as indicators	
Grade reduction for late papers	"Responsibility" grade is separate from content mastery grade (if assigned at all)
Zeroes for missing assignments	Students are given an "incomplete" for missing assignments with structured requirements to finish
Class notes and textbooks are used by students to make test/quiz corrections, and points are added back to their original score (with a ceiling on the revised grade)	Content is re-taught then re-assessed for mastery; mastery is demonstrated (not looked up), and the new grade replaces the old grade
Learning objectives written with a "degree" (Audience, behavior, condition, degree)	Learning targets and success criteria are used (I can, we will, we are learning to) with no set degrees of success
Points deducted on assignments for managerial tasks (such as name on paper, headings)	Point reduction is not used for compliance purposes
Participation grades assigned to encourage, reward, or punish students	Participation is not a graded activity
Grades used by teachers and/or students to set goals	Learning targets and level of mastery used to set goals
Grades given for practice work	Practice work used for formative assessment purposes and not graded
Trade and grade by students; teacher enters grade as is, never having seen the student's work	Self- and peer assessment with opportunity for revision; teacher uses evidence to provide ongoing feedback and is the final arbitrator of the grade
Rubrics created and used by teacher after students turn in work	Mastery criteria made clear in rubrics or scoring guide before students begin assignment
"Numerical Grade only" on returned papers	Success/intervention feedback provided on assignment with opportunity to correct for full credit

(*continued*)

Table 7.1 (continued)

A grade-oriented mentality	A learning-oriented mentality
Teacher (only) keeps track of grades	Students partner with the teacher in tracking their own progress in relation to the learning targets
Fixed mindset talk	Growth mindset talk
Grade distribution results in a bell-shaped curve	Goal is for all students to master all learning targets
Student questions as indicators	
Did I make a 100?	Did I get it all right?
Is this for a grade?	Will we assess my knowledge or skill on this?
How does my grade compare to my classmates?	How close am I to my learning goal?
Is it easy to make an A in this class?	Is this class a place where I will be able to learn?
How many points is this assignment worth?	How does completing this assignment fit in with our learning goals?
What can I do for extra credit?	What extra steps can I take to close the gap and show evidence of mastery?

If implemented correctly, SBG has the potential to make grade reporting an accurate representation of what students know and can do. In SBG, instead of offering only a single, overall grade for a course, teachers evaluate student mastery on different standards within a subject area, then report the grades separately. However, reporting grades on each standard would be cumbersome, therefore to streamline, strands or domains that represent broader themes could be grouped together. For example, in language arts students might receive separate marks for (1) Reading, (2) Writing, (3) Listening, (4) Speaking, and (5) Language skills (Guskey & Jung, 2012, p. 99). Thus, grade reports become more complex; however, they provide students and their parents a more detailed, informative report of student mastery. In addition, Guskey (p. 100) recommended that academic achievement grades (*product* criteria) be reported separately from non-academic factors such as class participation, attitude, effort, responsibility, and behavior (*process* criteria). Behavior is taken into account and reported to parents, but is separate from achievement, making it easier for teachers and students to pinpoint academic as well as behavioral strengths and weaknesses. During and after the transition to SBG, teachers may grapple with ways to induce unmotivated students to complete their work, point reductions no longer being an option. Using only classroom assessment events (rather than homework) to record evidence of mastery is one solution. And for those assignments that must be completed outside of class due to time restraints or the nature of the activity, students who return to class with unfinished work could be required to attend after-school tutorials, motivating them to finish on time in the future. Regardless, there are ways to hold students accountable and have them finish their work, other than using numerical grade reductions as leverage.

Unquestionably, SBG is more than an enhancement to our current grading system—it is one that calls for a significant paradigm shift in the mindsets of teachers and students alike. Schimmer in *Grading from the Inside Out* (2016) asserted that the standards-based mindset comprises three interconnected components. In an environment that uses standards-based learning and grading, teachers (1) give students full credit for what they know, not combining old evidence with new evidence, (2) redefine accountability, not punishing irresponsibility, and (3) repurpose the role of homework, using practice, formative assessment, and descriptive feedback to move the learning forward (p. 5). As far as students are concerned, SBG presents a novel culture of assessment that may be difficult for those students who have been experts at gaming the system. Vatterott (2015), much like Schimmer, outlined how SBG changes the grading game in four ways: (1) only learning is graded (no behavior included); (2) students are given multiple attempts after feedback to demonstrate mastery, while new information replaces old, and grades are not averaged together; (3) practice is not graded, but is used to check for understanding and feedback, and (4) penalties for late work may be included in a "work habits grade" but do not affect the student's academic grade. Within this system, cheating does nothing to help students learn or pass the class. The only way to win the game is to get better at learning (pp. 36 and 37).

SBG is gaining ground in classrooms across the county as individual teachers adopt new grading practices or as school districts adopt new grading policies. In an unofficial poll of approximately 300 Iowa school districts (Townsley, 2017), of the 126 secondary school respondents, 60 campuses (47.5%) reported that they were either at "beginning" (one or more teachers implementing with plans to scale further within the next 2 years), "almost" (implemented in some, but not all grade levels or content areas and a plan is in place to scale system-wide within the year), or "full" (implemented at all grade levels or content area) implementation levels, while 44 campuses (35%) were investigating SBG. Only 22 campuses (17.5%) indicated that they had no plan to investigate or implement SBG at their schools. This poll, although unscientific, is eye-opening and revealed a wave of interest that is gaining ground as school systems seek to find accurate grading and reporting systems.

In another study in Wisconsin (Larson, 2017), out of 510 high school principals surveyed, 86 responded to a poll designed to determine their levels of implementation relating to four features of SBG: (1) homework is not counted toward academic grade, (2) re-assessment is allowed on all summative assessments (no penalty), (3) behavior and life skills are reported separate from content grade, and (4) student proficiency against standards and learning targets makes up the academic grade. Of the 86 schools reporting, 8% met all four criteria, 10.4% met three of four, 29% met two of four, 48% met one of four, and 5% met none. Feature 2, allowing students to retake summative assessments with no grade penalty, was the most readily adopted practice for all respondents. Next was the practice of separating behavior from content on grade reporting (Feature 3). The most difficult and infrequently employed features reported by principals included the practice of *not* using homework toward academic grades (Feature 1) and using student proficiency against standards to make up their grade (Feature 4). These findings are consistent with other practitioners who claim difficulties in translating SBG into standards-based reporting and letting go of the practice of filling gradebooks with homework grades (using homework to teach *responsibility* as well). Although the sample size was small, this study sheds light on features of SBG that schools are likely to embrace and ones they may find difficult.

As a response to the problems inherent in our current system, some school districts are working to adopt competency-based education (CBE) that has the potential to move the system to a new level. CBE, referred to as mastery based, proficiency based, or performance based, replaces traditional education with structures that are learner centered and are designed to prepare students for success. High-quality CBE focuses, among other elements, on providing transferable and measurable learning goals that include the application and creation of knowledge and other twenty-first-century skills. The role of assessment is positive and empowering as it is individualized for students. CBE requires SBG to accommodate their goals of advancing students once they have demonstrated mastery. "Nearly every state has created some room for innovation that accommodates competency-based education, and competency-based systems are expanding across the country" (Lopez, Patrick, & Sturgis, 2017). To see an example of a school that has adopted CBE, see *Improving Assessment Through School on FIRE = Eminence Independent Schools, Kentucky* (https://sites.ed.gov/progress/2016/12/improving-assessment-through-school-on-fire-eminence-independent-schools-kentucky/), which serves as a model school that went from failing to excelling by creating a competency-based system that used SBG among the other learner-centered elements. Their school adopted a "learner-centric model that focuses on differentiated instruction, personalized learning, continuous growth, and the use of formative assessments and alternative means to assess student progress (e.g., photos, videos, audio, and samples of student work)."

In 2014, Eminence became the first district in Kentucky to reach 100 percent on the benchmarks for college and career readiness for their graduates on the state's accountability index. The district went from failing to meets state academic standards for many years to being in the top five percent of high schools in the State. Enrollment grew by 40 percent. Today, Eminence remains in the top five percent of high schools in the State—this, in a rural district where 64 percent of the students qualify for free and reduced-price lunch.

Eminence serves as a model of excellence and provides hope and encouragement for struggling school districts. Although representing a systems overhaul on a grand scale, taking smaller steps (yet still a bit daunting) such as changing grading systems has the potential to positively impact student learning. SBG implemented by individual teachers, cohorts of teachers, individual campuses, or in some cases as part of a district-wide initiative has made inroads into the learning landscape and shows promise but still is at some distance from large-scale application. For SBG to become part of the landscape:

1. Practical implementation logistics need to be refined and made more manageable
2. School administrators and teachers need training and support by an instructional leader who has successfully implemented SBG in the classroom
3. Parents and students need to be educated about the benefits of SBG and what the grades mean
4. Colleges and university admission requirements need to align with SBG and reporting

5. TPPs need to recognize the benefits of SBG and make it a part of teacher training, and
6. Teacher evaluation systems need to reflect the importance of accurate grading and reporting and be part of the goal setting process for teachers.

Teacher Preparation and Evaluation Systems

Teacher standards. Research studies validate the contributions that teaching standards make to improving student outcomes and how student outcomes should drive teacher standards:

> ...the linkage between teacher standards and student achievement is tight. The evidence of reverse causation suggests that the effect runs in both directions, showing both the effect of gain in the rigor of teacher standards on student achievement gains and the effect of student achievement gains on gains in the rigor teacher standards. This gives support for the standard driven as well as the performance-driven paths, implying that student performance drives teacher standards as much as (or more than) teacher standards drive student performance. (Lee, Liu, Amo, & Wang, 2014, p. 801)

This is an important piece of the big picture that may not be glamorous or exciting to address; nevertheless, it is important to the success of the whole. Although there are national organizations that provide teacher standards and board certifications, such as the National Board for Professional Teaching Standards, becoming board certified on a national scale is voluntary. Mandatory standards for teachers and TPPs are regulated by individual states and vary accordingly. ESSA relegated the regulation of TPPs to individual states, and as independent entities, they design and implement their own standards and assessment measures and provide oversight of programs that prepare teachers. These standards are established to ensure that teacher candidates have the requisite content and pedagogical knowledge and skills needed to become an effective classroom teacher.

If we aspire to instill, foster, and support constructivist teaching practices and to promote the use of formative assessment thus equipping and empowering students for the twenty-first century, then teaching standards should align with those desired outcomes. According to an Organisation for Economic Co-operation and Development (OECD) report (Ananiadou & Claro, 2009), very few countries have teaching standards that *focus* on twenty-first-century skills or training programs to support their implementation (p. 20); although, in most state standards, some skills can be found in combination with the myriad of competencies teacher candidates are expected to obtain. For example, a Texas competency (TExES PPR, Domain I, Competency 004:K) under the *Designing Instruction and Assessment to Promote Student Learning* domain requires that a pre-service teacher "understands the importance of self-directed learning and plans instruction and assessment that promote students' motivation and their sense of ownership of and responsibility for their own learning," aligning with the tenets of student-centered, self-directed learning. Other TExES competencies call for teachers to stimulate critical thinking and inquiry among students or provide instruction that ensures students apply metacognitive strategies—all desired learning outcomes. While higher-order skills are there, they do not take prominence. Additionally, the United States has National Educational Technology Standards (NETS) for teachers and school leaders that include more than simple foundational IT (information technology) skills expected of educators (Thomas & Knezek, 2008, p. 334), but retain an emphasis on technological capabilities, and as a result not explicitly addressing other twenty-first-century skills such critical thinking, communication, collaboration, and creativity and innovation, much less meta-layers of metacognition and systems-thinking and such.

I contend that TPPs should place a strong emphasis on preparing their pre-service teachers to equip and empower their future students for deep learning and the development of twenty-first-century skills as a necessary tool for understanding the content and its applicability, as well as preparing them to be problem solvers regardless of the content area. To prepare pre-service teachers for real-world demands, teacher standards and preparation programs need to align with findings from the learning sciences and explicitly address issues and practices that will enable them as teachers to prepare and guide their students toward a life of self-directed learning within a learner-centered environment.

Teacher preparation programs. Although many research studies have been conducted that compared the effectiveness of traditionally and alternatively certified teachers, few have been carried out that investigated how TPPs prepared teachers, or how they *should* prepare teachers, to meet the needs of twenty-first-century learners regardless of the route they take to certification. According to the National Research Council (2010),

TPPs are turning out more than 200,000 teachers every year and as decentralized entities are extremely diverse in many ways. TPPs are not always grounded in empirical research and tend to vary widely in mechanisms for accountability, lacking a cohesive, outcomes-driven accountability system. This provides an uneven playing field and elusive, dynamic targets for those engaged in the challenge of quality assurance within the teaching profession.

Regardless of the path that teachers take to certification, there are deep and enduring concepts about learners and learning that pre-service teachers need to understand and be able to apply as they venture into the classroom. It is a given that teachers need deep content and pedagogical content knowledge that they can use in a variety of contexts with a diversity of learners. Additionally, although not historically part of teacher education, TPPs should also equip their pre-service teachers with deep factual and conceptual knowledge about *how* students learn and how to apply that knowledge to the design and implementation of teaching and assessment frameworks. Explicitly teaching pre-service teachers the fundamentals of the learning sciences, including the power of metacognition, growth mindset, and other constructs that underlie learning, should be integral to teacher preparation curriculum, laying a firm foundation from which they can build.

Not only should pre-service teachers understand the science of learning, they should be prepared to pass that knowledge on to their students, not as a separate competency to be mastered but woven into the normal classroom practice of content learning. In my fledgling days as a high school biology teacher, I spent the first six weeks of the semester teaching students about lab safety followed by the scientific method. What a waste of precious time. Later, I learned to teach those two valuable concepts in the context of the content that we were learning at the time. Not only was it a more efficient use of time, but students understood them better as they connected the new knowledge and skills to existing knowledge and anchored them in a conceptual framework. Similarly, the same can be said for metacognitive and other twenty-first-century skills that are critical to students. They should not be taught in isolation but in the context of the content, deepening the learning while improving students' regulation of cognition and equipping them with skills that are needed for success.

Likewise, TPPs should develop dispositions of flexibility and adaptability in their pre-service teachers and instill in them a posture of life-long learning that will serve them throughout their career. Naturally, there are concrete knowledge and skills that pre-service teachers should possess before leaving TPPs, such as classroom management, technology use, lesson planning, and strategies to differentiate instruction, but those skills are secondary to the science of learning that will serve them throughout their careers as they adapt to the changing needs of students and the dynamic world of education.

Teacher evaluation systems. Becoming a high-quality, learner-centered teacher is rewarding in and of itself, but if teachers are evaluated, promoted, or compensated by a system of evaluation that is not compatible with learner-centered instruction, the process acts as an externally imposed factor that constrains rather than facilitates reform practices, including those of formative assessment. Teacher evaluations should be part of the process that empowers teachers in their own professional growth, focusing on student learning and teaching behaviors that get them there. The very term "evaluation" indicates a summative assessment of a teacher's performance, a measure of worth and competence, rather than a formative tool for growth.

For many years in the United States, despite good intentions of those who conceived and designed the instruments, teacher evaluations often ended up being of little consequence to those involved or were used for extrinsic purposes such as merit raises or compensation, promotion, or more often for documentation purposes to support termination. Traditional teacher-evaluation systems generally have been based on observations that were conducted on an annual basis (if that) and provided only a snapshot of teaching, focusing on what the teacher was doing rather than on the learner and learning. Teachers often planned an exceptional lesson in anticipation of the pre-arranged observation, making sure that they could check the criteria off their list (often derisively referred to as the production of a dog and pony show). Evaluations served the purpose of fulfilling a mandate by the state or federal government and were part of the teaching game, but rarely provided the feedback that teachers needed in order to improve classroom practice.

In the past few years, there has been a heightened awareness that teacher-evaluation systems are in disarray and in serious need of revamping. Most states are in the process of doing just that. The catalyst for such change comes, in part, as a result of strong federal incentives, including the Race to the Top initiative, and flexibility waivers, which began under NCLB, being intensified even more after ESSA shifted teacher-evaluation systems from federal to state control. The National Council on Teacher

Quality (2012) reported that 36 states and the District of Columbia have changed their teacher-evaluation policies since 2009 and include revisions to require annual teacher evaluations (currently 43 states), incorporate student achievement (32 states), differentiate levels of performance (26 states), conduct annual classroom observations (39 states), conduct multiple observations each year (22 states), and base tenure on performance (9 states). Developing new teacher-evaluation systems has been identified by scholars and policy makers alike as crucial to improving teacher quality and raising student academic performance across the country (McGuinn, 2012).

This begs the question of what kind of evaluation system Mary, Monica, and Phoebe needed in order to support their professional growth. Regardless of starting point and stage of career, all teachers need to be engaged in a cycle of collaborative, continuous improvement supported by a *professional growth and assessment system*—a more fitting title than "teacher evaluation." Although the system must provide a degree of evaluation for accountability and reporting purposes, the primary goal of a professional growth and assessment system should be to help teachers build capacity. In order to do so, they need to be immersed in a process:

- That utilizes PLCs or other professional development systems as a means to support the collaborative nature of learning about teaching, using the instrument as a framework
- In which learning targets are agreed upon, clear, measurable, achievable, and geared toward student growth and development; the learning targets are based on research of the learning sciences and are correlates of effective teaching
- In which teachers have a say in what progress looks like and what constitutes evidence of growth
- That is supported by ongoing feedback, modeling, and support from knowledgeable colleagues and an instructional leader
- That is collaborative and communal, where teachers learn from each other as well as from their students and their instructional leader
- In which teachers set challenging goals for growth and continually monitor their own progress, responding to feedback from their students, peers, and instructional leaders; and
- That requires teachers to keep track of and share their learning by providing evidence of their own growth as demonstrated by student learning outcomes.

- **As a side-note, many educators and policy makers call for an analysis of student learning gains as a measurement of teacher effectiveness. This value-added approach shows promise but continues to garner debate as it has limitations and problems with validity, accuracy, and reliability (Glazerman et al., 2011).

These design heuristics create a system of teacher evaluation that has the means to contribute significantly to improving what occurs in the classroom—empowering teachers in their craft. It is apparent, however, that few districts as they are currently structured have the capacity to implement, monitor, and support such system-wide, teacher-evaluation reform. Current structures that rely on the building principal to evaluate teachers are not sufficient to provide this level of sustained support. There are too many teachers and too few principals to make this a tenable and effective option. For this reason, instructional leaders need to be identified, developed, trained, and prepared to fill this role, unfortunately burdening the system with additional funding and staffing requirements, however.

Curriculum Standards and Testing

Curriculum standards, teacher standards, learning and assessment frameworks, and teacher and student evaluation processes and outcomes are all interrelated parts of learning ecosystems representing inputs, the black box of classroom practice, and outputs. It is essential that the interrelated parts of the system align and complement one another in order to offer a cohesive plan that results in the intended learning outcomes.

Curricular standards. Learner-centered environments that promote twenty-first-century skills call for standards that clearly articulate what it means for students to go beyond content knowledge to include application and transfer. Often called process standards, they should not stand alone but be embedded into the content standards representing ways that these skills can be used in the pursuit of content knowledge. For example, math process standards emphasize problem solving, reasoning and proof, communication, connections, and representations. Many states include process skills with their content standards, but teachers too often fail to emphasize them as learning activities are planned, making them an accidental product of the learning process rather than a purposeful goal. This phenomenon is due, in part, to the fact that these process skills are not necessarily tested, and as is commonly the case, "we do not teach what we do not test."

Secondly, the number of standards that teachers are expected to "cover" often leads to a cursory introduction to concepts, and under those circumstances, shallow learning takes place. Wiggins and McTighe described the habit of "coverage" as one of the twin sins of traditional design.

> A second form of aimlessness goes by the name of "coverage," an approach in which students march through a textbook, page by page (or teachers through lecture notes) in a valiant attempt to traverse all the factual material within a prescribed time. (Wiggins & McTighe, 2005, p. 16)

When state curriculum standards include a comprehensive laundry list of knowledge and skills that students are expected to master, overarching concepts, big ideas, and unifying themes get lost in the shuffle and teachers go straight to the checklist of mandated standards. They develop scope and sequence curricular plans to cover each and every topic and subsequently check them off their list as the year progresses and topics are covered. The long list of standards is virtually impossible to get through, much less teach with depth and apply process skills along the way. Some states have recognized the overabundance of standards that appear to be of the same value and have made adjustments. The state of Texas, for example, created categories of "supporting" and "readiness" standards to help teachers concentrate on elements that warrant more focused instruction—the readiness standards—enabling teachers to adjust lessons accordingly.

Policy makers and educators need to agree on unifying themes and big ideas that are fundamental to each discipline and combine those with process and self-regulatory skills that prepare students to have a deep foundational content knowledge and the ability to transfer that knowledge to real-world situations (termed "knowledge in use"). Equally important, standards should address fewer and more salient concepts and focus on core ideas—those that have broad implications within or across the discipline. An exemplary model that embodies these ambitious goals includes the Next Generation Science Standards (NGSSs), which are emphasized in the National Research Council's *Framework for K–12 Science Education* (NRC, 2012).

The National Research Council's Framework for K–12 Science Education (NRC, 2012) puts forth a new vision of science education where students engage in science and engineering practices to develop and use disciplinary core ideas (DCIs) and crosscutting concepts to explain phenomena and solve problems. These three dimensions work together to help students build an integrated understanding of a rich network of connected ideas. The more connections developed, the greater the ability of students to solve problems, make decisions, explain phenomena, and make sense of new information. (Krajcik, Codere, Dahsah, Bayer, & Mun, 2014, p. 158)

The *Framework* and related NGSSs alleviate the burden of coverage, focusing on engaging in science and engineering practices to develop and use disciplinary core ideas (DCIs) and crosscutting concepts (those that serve as intellectual tools for connecting important ideas across all science disciplines, sometimes referred to as unifying themes) to explain phenomena and solve problems engaging in the processes of science (Krajcik et al., 2014, p. 158). Because of the nature of the DCI and crosscutting concepts, the knowledge that students gain from the learning experiences are transferable to other scientific phenomena and problems. The standards are expressed as Performance Expectations (PEs) that blend the three dimensions (DCIs, crosscutting concepts, and science and engineering practices) together in a manner that requires students to transfer their knowledge or demonstrate knowledge in use. PEs cannot be achieved through passive learning—listening to lectures or traditional instruction—but rather requires a systematic process of learner-centered activities that allows students to build explanations and propose solutions to problems.

Testing and accountability. Testing and accountability will always be a substantial and potent element that affects the learning ecosystem with which we must contend. Standardized tests, if leveraged to the benefit of learning, have the potential to provide useful information about students, school systems, and the nation's progress toward reform as we work to be more competitive in a global society.

The usefulness of large-scale, standardized tests should not be underestimated, but they require a cohesive and coherent method of determining levels of student mastery, which contemporary systems lack. Part of the problem is the tightrope that is walked, balancing local and state autonomy with the need for federal oversight. Individual states have been given more flexibility on *how* to measure student learning under new ESSA guidelines, yet federal mandates remain, and states must maintain a system of accountability in which they test, disaggregate, and report data on student performance. Systems vary widely from state to state, and efforts at centralization have been met with strong and persistent resistance, making it unlikely that the United States will ever have a high degree of centralization. The resistance became evident in the early 1990s when the US Senate rejected a set of national history standards supported and funded by the federal government under President George H.W. Bush and continues to be an issue with which we contend to this day. As an illustration, in response to indicators that the United States lags behind other developed countries (due, in part, to the mixed bag of academic standards that vary from state to state), a coalition emerged that sought to address our disappointing level of achievement compared to other developed countries. In 2009, Common Core standards (CCSs) in the English Language Arts and mathematics were developed by the National Governors Association (NGA) along with the Council of Chief State School Officers (CCSSO) and the nonprofit education reform group Achieve. They were designed to prepare students to succeed in entry level careers, introductory academic college courses, and workforce training programs. The CCSs claimed to be aligned with college and career expectations and based on rigorous content and application of knowledge through higher-order thinking skills. Although adopted by 46 states in the beginning, a great deal of misinformation, confusion, and political influences caused many states to repeal or withdraw adoption, or at the very least, revise and rename the much maligned and hotly debated standards.

During the rise of CCSs, educators recognized the need for tests that measured student success in achieving the national standards and, as a result, the US Department of Education awarded two assessment consortia $330 million in Race to the Top competitive grants to develop assessments aligned to the standards. At one point, almost all states had joined one or both of the major consortia (the *Partnership for Assessment of Readiness for College and Careers* or *PARCC* and the *Smarter Balanced Assessment Consortium* or *SBAC*). These testing initiatives, much like the standards, have proven unpopular as a large number of participating states dropped out. Unfortunately, states tend to be highly suspicious of federal entities and are strongly drawn to local control, often dismissing research-based practices on political or ideological grounds in pursuit of their own autonomy.

Ultimately, efforts of devising a cohesive, coherent system of testing in the United States that assesses deep learning and knowledge in practice are unlikely, but the efforts to develop better tests should not be abandoned.

If we want teachers to teach for depth and transferability with an emphasis on twenty-first-century skills that students need, not only do we need to devise new standards, we need tests that measure student success based on those standards.

Likewise, it should be noted that there are positive aspects to testing that are often overlooked. Benjamin and Pashler (2015) supported the practice of standardized tests, claiming that there exists great potential in tests as tools for learning and not just tools for evaluation of achievement. Existing literature revealed that frequent testing (1) results in an improved memory of the tested material and the ability to recall the material again later, (2) decreases the rate at which material is forgotten, (3) improves the ability to generalize and apply knowledge, (4) encourages the kind of thinking that is essential not just for retention but also for mentally organizing the acquisition of new material, (5) allows leaners to segregate their learning and prevent confusion among topics, and (6) reveals what students know and do not know, thus providing the opportunity for feedback that can be used to fine-tune knowledge. It turns out then, that testing can have benefits to learning.

The use of testing for accountability measures is not the problem, therefore, but rather the design of tests and what they tend to measure is. Historically, large-scale, standardized tests have measured declarative knowledge, which is no longer the point of schooling as students have information at their fingertips due to the availability of technology. Testing formats, time restraints, and limitations on resources make factual recall the most expedient thing to test, given our current systems. However, new tests are emerging that have promise and can be administered at scale. According to the NRC (2013, p. 145), the computerized, problem-solving component of the PISA offers a format where items are grouped in units around a common problem. The problems are presented within realistic, everyday contexts, such as refueling a moped, playing on a handball team, mixing elements in a chemistry lab, or taking care of a pet. The difficulty of the items is manipulated by increasing the number of variables or the number of relationships that the test taker has to deal with. Scoring of the items involves four components of problem solving: (1) information retrieval, (2) model building, (3) forecasting, and (4) monitoring and reflecting (p. 145). Another example of improved testing is provided by an exam created by the National Council of Bar Examiners that effectively measures a student's ability to transfer what he or she knows in order to practice law.

These and other promising examples each start with a strong model of the competencies to be assessed; use simulated cases and scenarios to pose problems that require extended analysis, evaluation, and problem solving; and apply sophisticated scoring models to support inferences about student learning. The PISA example, in addition, demonstrates the dynamic and interactive potential of technology to simulate authentic problem-solving situations. (p. 146)

Conclusion

Classroom teachers have the opportunity to be agents of change, but in order to do so, externally imposed elements such as grading systems, teacher preparation and evaluation systems, and curricular standards and high-stakes testing must be supportive, not constraining. These interrelated elements represent parts of a whole system that are critical to its success and must be addressed if the United States plans to remain competitive in a global society. The learning sciences present evidence of how students learn and identify the learning environments that support their growth, now it is up to policy makers and educators to leverage that knowledge to the benefit of our students, and therefore to society as a whole.

Works Cited

Ananiadou, K., & Claro, M. (2009). *21st century skills and competences for new millennium learners in OECD countries*. Paris OECD Publishing.

Benjamin, A. S., & Pashler, H. (2015). The value of standardized testing: A perspective from cognitive psychology. *Policy Insights from the Behavioral and Brain Sciences, 2*(1), 13–23.

National Research Council. (2010). *Preparing teachers: Building evidence for sound policy*. Washington, DC: The National Academies Press.

National Research Council. (2012). *A framework for K-12 science education: Practices, crosscutting concepts, and core ideas*. Washington, DC: The National Academies Press.

National Research Council. (2013). *Education for life and work: Developing transferable knowledge and skills in the 21st century*. Washington, DC: The National Academies Press.

Glazerman, S., Goldhaber, D., Loeb, S., Raudenbush, S., Staiger, D. O., Whitehurst, G. J., & Croft, M. (2011). *Passing muster: Evaluating teacher evaluation systems* (pp. 1–36). Washington: Brooking Institution.

Guskey, T. R., & Jung, L. A. (2012). *Answers to essential questions about standards, assessments, grading, and reporting*. Thousand Oaks, CA: Corwin Press.

Krajcik, J., Codere, S., Dahsah, C., Bayer, R., & Mun, K. (2014). Planning instruction to meet the intent of the next generation science standards. *Journal of Science Teacher Education, 25*(2), 157–175.

Larson, G. L. (2017). *An evaluation of standards-based grading and reporting in Wisconsin high schools* (Doctor of Education), The University of Wisconsin Oshkosh, Unpublished dissertation.

Lee, J., Liu, X., Amo, L. C., & Wang, W. L. (2014). Multilevel linkages between state standards, teacher standards, and student achievement: Testing external versus internal standards-based education models. *Educational Policy, 28*(6), 780–811.

Lopez, N., Patrick, S., & Sturgis, C. (2017). *Quality and equity by design: Charting the course for the next phase of competency-based education.* iNACOL CompetencyWorks.

Marzano, R. J. (2011). *Formative assessment and standards-based grading.* Bloomington, IN: Solution Tree Press.

McGuinn, P. (2012). *The state of teacher evaluation reform: State education agency capacity and the implementation of new teacher-evaluation systems.* Center for American Progress.

Schimmer, T. (2016). *Grading from the inside out.* Bloomington, IN: Solution Tree Press.

Thomas, L. G., & Knezek, D. G. (2008). Information, communications, and educational technology standards for students, teachers, and school leaders. In *International handbook of information technology in primary and secondary education* (pp. 333–348). Springer.

Townsley, M. (2017). *Secondary standards-based grading in Iowa.* Retrieved from https://sites.google.com/view/iowasbg/home

Vatterott, C. (2015). *Rethinking grading: Meaningful assessment for standards-based learning.* Alexandria, VA: ASCD.

Wiggins, G., & McTighe, J. (2005). *Understanding by design* (2nd ed.). Alexandria, VA: Association for Supervision and Curriculum Development.

Index

A
Accountability, 1–20, 50, 76, 82, 84, 90, 91, 99, 136, 138, 158, 161, 163, 166, 168, 171–173
Achievement tests, 9, 19
African Americans, 2, 3, 15
Alternative certification program (ACP), 59, 65, 110, 111
American Association for the Advancement of Science (AAAS), 13
Apprenticeships, 2, 3
Assessment as learning, 41
Assessment *for* learning (AfL), 25, 26, 41, 131
Assessment *of* learning, 26
Assessment Training Institute (ATI), 14

B
Backwards design, 33, 131, 143–145
Behaviorism, 17, 36
Behavior over time (BOT) graph, 141, 142
Biological Sciences Curriculum Study (BSCS), 13, 14

Black, Paul, 13, 14, 17, 25, 28, 43
Bush, George H. W., 16, 172
Bush, George W., 16

C
Case or theoretical knowledge, 79
Civil Rights Act, 15
Classroom teacher
  beliefs, 77–81
  forms of knowledge, 82, 86, 89, 100, 101
  professional development of, 80, 105, 114
  teacher capacity, 131, 136, 148
  teacher credentialing (certifications), 105, 107
  teacher effect, the, 75, 76
  teacher evaluation systems, 164, 167, 168
  teacher institutes, 110
  teacher leaders, 136, 139
  teacher preparation, 80, 105, 112, 123, 155, 164–169, 174
Clinton, Bill, 16
Cognitive science, 17, 105, 120, 133

Coleman Report, 15
Collaboration, 29, 36, 87, 90, 99, 114, 133, 145, 165
Colonial period, 1, 105
Committee of Ten, 9, 112
Common Core standards (CCSs), 172
Common School period, 4, 80
Comprehensive high school, 10, 106
Concept or causal mapping, 141
Conceptual change, 76, 117, 121, 139, 140, 146
Conformative assessment, 41
Constructivism, 5, 11, 33, 36, 37, 73
Contemplative learning, 149
Content knowledge, 63, 64, 93, 95, 102, 105, 119, 124, 126, 133, 134, 137, 143, 147, 169, 170
Coverage, 90, 170, 171

D

Dame schools, 2
Deep learning, 17, 134, 149, 155, 165, 172
De-formative assessment, 41
Deliberate practice, 133, 148
Dewey, John, 5, 6, 126
Direct instruction, 8, 72, 113
Discovery learning, 33, 142
Dweck, Carol, 38, 39, 120, 149, 150

E

Early National period, 2
Educational Testing Service (ETS), 13, 14, 115
Education for All Handicapped Children Act (EAHCA), 15
Education Next, 19
Educator certification program (ECPs), 40, 111, 112
Elementary and Secondary Education Act (ESEA), 11, 15–17

Entity theory of intelligence, 120
  by students, 120
  by teachers, 120 (*see also* Fixed mindset)
Equal Educational Opportunity Survey (EEOS), 15
Every Student Succeeds Act (ESSA), 11, 17, 110, 164, 167, 171
Experiential learning, 33, 149

F

Federal role in education, 11
Feedback, 13, 14, 25, 26, 29, 30, 33–35, 39, 41, 43, 54, 56, 64, 67, 68, 70, 72, 89, 91, 95, 99, 118, 135, 140, 144–148, 151, 161, 167, 168, 173
Feedback loops, 141
5E learning cycle, 33, 146
Fixed mindset, 39, 90, 150, 158
Flipped learning, 33
Folk pedagogy, 27, 40, 78, 79, 89, 94, 97, 101, 123
Formative assessment
  defined, 25, 26
  in the classroom, 12, 25, 32, 35, 42, 44, 72, 82, 131
  problems with, 25, 27, 29, 36, 42, 133
  the purpose of, 13, 25, 26, 28, 37, 85, 86, 118, 126, 131
Forms of knowledge, 80, 82, 86, 89, 100, 101, 124
Franklin, Benjamin, 2, 113

G

Goal setting
  by students, 30, 145
  by teachers, 30, 144, 146, 148, 164
  importance of, 148, 164

Goals 2000, 16
Grade-oriented mentality, 158, 160
Growth mindset, 39, 40, 56, 133, 134, 143, 149–151, 166

H
Harris, William Torrey, 7
Harvard's Program on Education Policy and Governance, 19
High-stakes testing, 15–18, 44, 82, 84, 133, 155, 158, 174

I
Incremental theory of intelligence, 38
  in students, 118, 149
  in teachers, 118, 122
  See also Growth mindset
Individuals with Disabilities Education Act (IDEA), 16
Industrialization, 4, 9, 19
Informal education, 2
Informal schools, 11
Inquiry-based learning, 33, 94, 95, 97
INSET model of professional development, 114
Instructionism, 4–6, 9, 11, 12, 17, 18, 35, 40
Instructivism, 73, 94
IQ testing, 7

J
James, William, 6
Jefferson, Thomas, 2, 3
Jim Crow laws, 4, 10
Johnson, Lyndon B., 10, 11

K
Kelly, Frederick J., 9
Knowledge economy, 19, 124, 126, 133

L
Laboratory schools, 6
Lancaster, Joseph, 3
Learner-centered instruction, 6, 9, 11, 39, 42, 98, 101, 140, 146, 149, 158, 167
Learning goals, 28, 30, 31, 33, 35, 37, 39, 43, 71, 88, 121, 133, 136, 137, 139, 145, 158, 162
Learning-oriented mentality, 159–160
Learning sciences, 17, 37, 40, 131, 143, 149, 165, 166, 168, 174
Learning trajectory-based instruction, 121, 122
Lesson analysis protocol, 147

M
Mann, Horace, 4, 6, 7
Mastery learning, 41, 43
Mental model of learning, 88, 120–122, 140
Metacognition, 28, 71, 134, 150, 151, 165, 166
Metacognitive awareness inventory (MAI), 28
Modern period, 10
Monitorial schools, 3, 4

N
National Academy for Curriculum Leadership (NACL), 14
National Assessment of Educational Progress (NAEP), 15
National Defense Education Act (NDEA), 15
National Research Council (NRC), 13, 14, 17, 19, 124, 126, 134, 166, 170, 171, 173
National Science Teachers Association (NSTA), 13, 14
A Nation at Risk, 16

Neuromyths, 121
Neuroplasticity, 37, 120
Neurosciences, 17, 37, 120, 121, 148
Next Generation Science Standards (NGSS), 170, 171
Nixon, Richard, 12
No Child Left Behind (NCLB), 11, 16, 50, 114, 115, 167
Normal schools, 106, 107, 110

O
Obama, Barack, 17
Orientations, 38, 41, 119, 120

P
Papert, Seymour, 4
Parker, Francis, 5
Pedagogical content knowledge, 52, 77, 78, 114, 122, 138, 147, 166
Pedagogical knowledge, 78, 123, 164
Peer-assessment, 33, 43, 145
Performance goals, 30, 39, 90
Personal practice assessment theories (PPATs), 49, 52, 60, 66, 77, 81–101, 122, 155
Personal practice theories (PPTs), 76–82, 118
Pestalozzi, Johann, 5, 6
Piaget, Jean, 11, 12
Practice-centered inquiry (PCI), 6, 30, 76, 89, 91, 97, 99, 102, 135, 139, 140, 145, 149
Practice schools, 5
Problem-based learning, 33, 149
Professional development
  cascading, 139
  conceptual change, 121
  consensus view, 116
  ineffectiveness, 118
  measuring effectiveness, 116, 118
Professional learning community (PLC), 132, 136–146, 148, 151, 168
Program logic model, 141
Programme for International Student Assessment (PISA), 19, 173, 174
Progressive period, 7, 8, 156
Propositional knowledge, 78, 79, 89, 94–96, 101, 123

R
Race to the Top, 167, 172
Reflection
  by students, 31, 80, 95
  by teachers, 33, 80, 81, 123, 135, 139, 147
  importance of, 123
Rural schools, 9, 107, 110

S
Science of learning, 17, 36, 121, 133, 143, 148–151, 166, 167
  See also Learning sciences, the
Science Teachers Learning through Lesson Analysis (STeLLA), 147
Scientific movement, 9
Scriven, Michael, 12
Self-assessment, 13, 30, 34, 42, 146, 147
Self-directed learning, 13, 165
Self-fulfilling prophesy, 119
Self-regulated learning, 28, 149
Service learning, 149
Seven Cardinal Principles, 10
Sheldon, Edward, 5
Sputnik, 10, 15, 16, 113
Standards based grading (SBG), 158, 162
Strategic knowledge, 78, 79, 89, 90, 101, 102, 122, 123, 138, 145, 148, 151, 155

Student achievement, 13, 15, 19–20, 38, 43, 75, 76, 110, 116, 118, 136, 158, 164, 168
Systems thinking, 140, 165

T
Taylor, Frederick W., 8
Taylorism, 8, 18, 110, 156
Teacher-centered instruction, 18
Teacher preparation program (TPPs), 110, 112, 164–167
Team-based learning, 149
Test autopsy, 31
Thorndike, Edward, 6–8
Traditional instruction, 1, 35, 56, 72, 80, 89, 90, 94, 99, 158, 171
Traffic light activity, 29
Transfer, 56, 64, 88, 89, 126, 134, 139, 146, 169–171, 173

Transmission model of teaching, 37
21st century skills, 125, 126, 133, 155, 162, 165, 166, 169, 173

V
Video analysis, 145, 147
Vygotsky, Lev, 36, 39, 88

W
Webster, Noah, 2
Westward expansion, 4
Wiliam, Dylan, 13, 14, 17, 25, 28, 35, 43, 76, 144
Women's colleges, 106

Z
Zone of proximal development (ZPD), 29, 36, 89